Twayne's United States Authors Series

EDITOR OF THIS VOLUME

David J. Nordloh

Indiana University

Stephen Crane

Revised Edition

Stephen Crane

STEPHEN CRANE

By EDWIN H. CADY

Duke University

REVISED EDITION

TWAYNE PUBLISHERS

A DIVISION OF G. K. HALL & CO., BOSTON

(Street)

PS1449
.C85Z575
1980

Library of Congress Cataloging in Publication Data

Cady, Edwin Harrison.
Stephen Crane.

(Twayne's United States authors series ;   TUSAS 23)
Bibliography: p. 169 - 71
Includes index.
1.   Crane, Stephen, 1871 - 1900—
Criticism and interpretation.
PS1449.C85Z575   1980   813'.4   79-26608
ISBN 0-8057-7299-5

For Fran

Contents

About the Author

Edwin H. Cady began to specialize in American Literature while taking his A.B. degree from Ohio Wesleyan University (1939). He continued through the M.A. at the University of Cincinnati (1940) and the Ph.D. at the University of Wisconsin (1943). He has held teaching posts at Wisconsin, Ohio State, Syracuse, and Indiana and taught overseas as a Smith-Mundt professor at Uppsala, Sweden (1951 - 52) and as a Fulbright visitor to Japanese universities and the Kyoto Seminar (1967). A member of the University Press boards at Syracuse and subsequently Indiana, he became a founding member of the Center for Editions of American Authors and the first General Editor of *A Selected Edition of W. D. Howells*. Cady is presently Chairman of the Board of Editors of the journal *American Literature*. Among other activities, he has served on the United States Commission for UNESCO (1969 - 71), chaired the athletics committees of both Duke and Indiana, and represented each in its respective Conference as well as the NCAA. He has published a number of books and articles on American writers, including Stephen Crane, and worked on both NET programs and educational films. He is currently Andrew W. Mellon Professor in the Humanities at Duke University.

Preface

The reader whose attention is solicited to a Revised Edition has a right to be told, at least briefly, from the outset what is the news. In the case of Stephen Crane it is that what was twenty years ago something like a frontier, sparsely and unevenly inhabited, uncertainly developed, has been largely occupied. Crane is now an established, major American author, a specialty, a "field" with a gigantic CEAA Edition and a secondary bibliography so large it has called forth half a dozen surveys of itself. This edition attempts to interpret at large the new, highly developed, but by no means stable situation.

Nevertheless, the book has insisted upon remaining what it always was—a study of Stephen Crane and his work in preference to an overview of the field. It devotes attention, displaying some evidence not heretofore generally known, of the historiographical elusiveness and instability of much of what has passed for "evidence" in Crane studies. But it undertakes to treat illustratively as well as critically of such matters more by brief example than by long, thorough examination because it must save its space for Crane. It tries to clarify terminological problems, especially Crane and "the Christian gentleman," which have bothered some earlier readers.

Its major illumination of Crane's work, the central issue, however, comes from a correction of the volume's earlier perception of *Maggie, a Girl of the Streets*. The 1893 text, particularly as presented by Joseph Katz and Maurice Bassan, brought the critic to views of *Maggie* not only radically different from those of the first edition but, so far as he knows, different from those available elsewhere in the body of Crane criticism.

Edwin H. Cady

Duke University

Acknowledgments

In addition to the Crane specialists acknowledged in the "Notes and References" and bibliographical essays, I am particularly grateful to Norma W. Cady, who worked, coped, and above all understood, as she always does; to the lady to whom this book is dedicated, whose friendship I value increasingly with the years; to Richard Baldwin, E. Fred Carlisle, and Michael Fowler, for paid research assistance; to James M. Cox, the late Albert J. George, Terence Martin, Jack Lunn Mowers, the late Lester G. Wells, and to William E. Wilson for reading the manuscript. In the years since publication of the first version of this book I have learned much about Crane from Joseph M. Katz. For their active, generous help, and particularly now for the Linson/Mowers photographs, I am grateful to the Stephen Crane Collection, Lena R. Arents Rare Book Room, Syracuse University Library; the staffs and collections of the Clifton Waller Barrett Collection, Alderman Library, University of Virginia; the Lilly and University Libraries, Indiana University; the Houghton Library, Harvard University; and the Columbia University Library.

For a grant for research travel and assistance in the preparation of the first edition from the Graduate Research Division of the Indiana University Graduate School, the late John W. Ashton, Dean and Vice-President, is once more gratefully acknowledged.

Permissions

For permission to quote copyrighted or otherwise privileged materials, thanks are hereby extended to the following: Alfred A. Knopf, Inc., holder of the literary rights to Stephen Crane's letters, manuscripts, etc., for general permission to quote from such materials and, more specifically, for permission to quote from Thomas Beer, *Stephen Crane*, 1923; and Robert W. Stallman, ed., *Stephen Crane: An Omnibus*, 1952. The Syracuse University Press, for permission to quote from Edwin H. Cady and Lester G. Wells, eds., *Stephen Crane's Love Letters to Nellie Crouse*, 1954; Melvin Schoberlin, ed., *The Sullivan County Sketches of Stephen Crane*, 1949; Corwin K. Linson, *My Stephen Crane*, 1958. The New York University Press for permission to quote from Robert W. Stallman and Lillian Gilkes, *Stephen Crane: Letters*, 1960. Also to the Syracuse University Library for permission to publish the Linson/Mowers photographs; to the Clifton Waller Barrett Collection of the Alderman Library, the University of Virginia for permission to examine and quote from the manuscript of *The Red Badge of Courage* and Stephen Crane's pocket notebook; and to the Lilly Library, Indiana University for permission to quote the corrected inscription on the cover of Hamlin Garland's copy of the first edition of *Maggie;* to *ELH* and the Johns Hopkins Press for permission to reprint from my article "Stephen Crane and 'the Strenuous Life' "; and to the Trustees of the Remington Art Memorial, Ogdensburg, New York, for the letter of Frederic Remington to W. D. Howells.

Chronology

1871   Stephen Crane born November 1, in Newark, New Jersey, fourteenth and last child of the Rev. Dr. Jonathan Townley Crane and Mary Helen Peck Crane.

1878   Dr. Crane assumes Methodist pastorate in Port Jervis, New York; Stephen begins his first schooling in the town which would become his "Whilomville."

1880   Jonathan Townley Crane dies, February 16.

1883   Mrs. Crane moves with Stephen to Asbury Park, New Jersey.

1888   Stephen enrolls as student at Hudson River Institute [and Claverack College], Claverack, New York. In summer begins to assist brother Townley Crane with his Press Bureau at Asbury Park.

1890   Stephen enters Lafayette College as engineering student, September 12; joins Delta Upsilon fraternity; fails course and leaves after Christmas vacation.

1891   Registers, January 9, at Syracuse University; plays catcher and shortstop on varsity baseball team; reports for newspapers; attends few classes. In summer meets Hamlin Garland after reporting Garland lecture on realism. Does not return to college in fall but tries to establish self in New York City. Mary Helen Peck Crane dies, December 7.

1892   Fails to hold newspaper jobs. Publication of some "Sullivan County Sketches."

1893   Private printing, paid for by Crane, of *Maggie: A Girl of the Streets*; through Garland, gains friendship of W. D. Howells. Begins *The Red Badge of Courage*.

1894   Begins writing poems. Begins *George's Mother*. "An Experiment in Misery" and "An Experiment in Luxury" published. *The Red Badge* published (abridged) by Bacheller Syndicate in newspapers.

1895   Crane starts West to report for Bacheller. Final revision of *The Red Badge* made in New Orleans; to Mexico, March

12. *The Black Riders* published May 11. *The Red Badge of Courage* published October 5; by December, Crane an international literary celebrity.

1896   *George's Mother*; *Maggie*; *The Little Regiment*; *The Third Violet*, various other stories and some poems all published. Crane becomes butt of envious, malicious gossip in New York: the Dora Clark case makes him victim of persecution by police; to Jacksonville, Florida, as correspondent to Cuban insurrection, November; meets Cora Taylor.

1897   January 2, shipwrecked from *Commodore* off Florida coast; "The Open Boat" published June. To Greece (accompanied by Cora Taylor) to report Turkish war (April - May). To England, with Cora as "Mrs. Crane"; writes "The Monster," "The Bride Comes to Yellow Sky," "Death and the Child." Meets Joseph Conrad.

1898   *The Open Boat and Other Tales of Adventure*. To the United States to volunteer for Spanish-American war service; rejected by Navy, goes as war correspondent for Pulitzer; involves self as daringly as possible in combat action at Guantanamo, Cuzco, Las Guasimas, San Juan Hill; writes some of war's best dispatches; invalided home and discharged, returns at once for Hearst to Puerto Rico; "disappears" into Havana. To New York in November.

1899   To England where Cora had manorial "Brede Place" and a mountain of their debts waiting for him; writes desperately to catch up. *War Is Kind*; *Active Service*; *The Monster and Other Stories* published. At big Christmas Week houseparty Crane suffers massive tubercular hemorrhage.

1900   *Whilomville Stories*; *Wounds in the Rain*; *Great Battles of the World* published. Crane works on *The O'Ruddy* (finished by Robert Barr, 1903) and the pieces which appeared as *Last Words*, 1902. Dies, Badenweiler, Germany, June 5.

CHAPTER 1

The Elusive Stephen Crane

"After all, I cannot help vanishing and disappearing and dissolving. It is my foremost trait."[1]

CRANE for many years enjoyed a reputation at which he would have been amused. He held the American record for periodically rediscovered unknown geniuses. The present situation, I suspect, would have sent him into a gale of ironic glee. Not only a major, standard author, he has become a scholarly field with specialists. Yet the field illustrates Crane's perception that life is war.

As he once explained, he slid through the world unexplained—always elusive. Even to good friends Crane appeared to pass through his time like a visitant from outer space. The solid facts about him are brief; what ought to be solid facts are in some essentials as obscure, the reasons for his brilliance as conjectural as the annals of a comet. Though he was the first modern writer on the American scene, it is surprising to realize how much we still do not know about him. The dates and therefore the sequences of some of his most crucial acts and writings remain shadowy. We know little about his reading. Many key anecdotes rest upon undocumentable hearsay or long-delayed reminiscence. Too many are contradictory or otherwise dubious. Therefore much of what is understood about Stephen Crane remains conjectural, possibly absurd. He has been a handy peg upon which to hang pet theories or myths.

Coming back to Crane in the round roughly twenty years after, what is there to say? What does one see and feel? Certainly he has changed. Larger and more prominent in reputation, more exactly defined, he also seems, paradoxically, shrunken. We know his limits more precisely. Certain potentialities imaginable when they seemed to loom through the mists of the half-known diminish in the sharp relief of clearer light. Crane is an established genius with a first-rate canon forever small because he died young. Though he remains elusive, perhaps always will, perhaps that will be most essentially because, as W. D. Howells shrewdly observed, Crane had not yet come into the mystery of himself before Christmas 1899. And, though mist and shadow still lie about him, no unglimpsed masterpiece is likely to emerge from it. We have Crane—if we can catch him.

Occasional evidence appears to confirm the long-standing suspicion that hitherto sequestered manuscripts, notebooks, and letters—perhaps a little newspaper writing not yet identified—will pop up. I am now convinced—as I became, correctly, long ago about Howells—that no substantial change will result when presently sequestered materials transpire. Their effect will be to enrich the ground for understanding what we already know.

Much notable work has been done. Great collectors, especially Clifton Waller Barrett, and the great research libraries have given us much new primary material. The work of scholars like Lester Wells, who founded the modern era, Schoberlin and Colvert and Gilkes and Fryckstedt, and more recently Katz and Bruccoli and Gullason, have sifted through most if not all of the probably rewarding archaeological digs. Singly and in collaboration, Professor Robert W. Stallman has performed heroic deeds. To all that must be added the achievement of Professor Fredson Bowers and his staff in preparing the *Virginia Edition*.

Much of course remains to be done, but the problems have passed into the hands of sophisticated and prolific (though often quarrelsome) specialists. It would be fair to say of American literary studies generally that what was once notoriously an Age of Criticism—perhaps too much characterized by the free-standing explication—has become now largely an Age of Bibliographies. In this our Alexandrian time the Crane industry is as replete with surveys and selections of past commentary, editions, case books, anthologies, and gatherings of raw materials for scholarship as any author field. The Crane canon seems pretty well set. Criticism has recurrently agreed that the quality of Crane's vision, like his irony, stands at the center of what matters. Critics still muster the "isms" and drill them, sometimes in variant formations, on the old paradeground. But it is really a rather long time since anything significantly new stepped forward in Crane criticism.

It would have been a cause for joy, when the basic work for the first edition of this volume was being done, to know that the Crane field would spring into being so massively populated, so industrious. And yet, after those strenuous years, Crane remains elusive, his mystery not penetrated. Why not? The answer, as usual, seems complex.

To read again through the file of Professor Joseph Katz's wonderful *Stephen Crane Newsletter* (1966 - 1970) is to see how richly the field burgeoned, how marvelously it promised. One powerful name after another appeared in the lengthening "Quarterly Check-list" of newly published or newly announced intentions of Crane work. Every issue seemed to print one if not seven additions or corrections to the *Letters*. The promise of Stallman's biography, bibliography, and editing projects sounded ever larger and better. The *Virginia Edition* was announced. A golden age seemed at hand.

But soon, by 1968, one could see dismay commence to spread as the long-advertised volumes began actually to appear. A record of disillusion is plain in the *Newsletter*, which also records commentary which appeared elsewhere. It is writ large: he who runs may read.

In fact, it was to become the fate of the *Crane Newsletter* to trace the rise, truncated peak, and decline of Crane studies in half a decade. Beginning late during the brief Age of Affluence in American humanistic studies, the *Newsletter* built up momentum enough to carry it almost through the subsequent Time of Troubles so nearly fatal to those same studies. The last number in my collection is Volume V, no. 1, Fall 1970, and it was postmarked 30 May 1972. Though its own contents were fairly well up to standard, the "Quarterly Checklist" had shrunk to seven items. The cover reproduced Linson's India-ink brush sketch of Crane going West, looking remarkably like a prescience of Charlie Chaplin's "Little Tramp" about to shuffle into a cinematic fade-out, eluding us again.

What, then, keeps Stephen Crane so elusive? Aside from the insoluble problems arising from the parsimony of fate in killing him off so early, I think the problems are three: (1) personal failings in people; (2) exasperating gaps and unreliability in primary evidence; (3) failures, often incredible, in scholarly responsibility. Too much of what we know about Crane stems from a journalist like Thomas Beer or a poet like John Berryman who could not much trouble himself over so dry, so pedantic a matter as the rules of evidence. Too much more stems from the work of scholars temperamentally unable to shoulder the burdens of accuracy and responsibility.

As one notably civilized scholar remarked years ago, there seem to be qualities possessed by certain authors which are traceable in the emotional characteristics of their scholars. If that be so, he said, there must have been an angry, daffy side to Crane—his famous *méfiance*, perhaps—which exhibits itself in Craneans. In the last consideration, it is so hard to deal with the "hit-list of my enemies" variety of comment without coming to share in it that it seems best on the whole to let it pass. Why should essays in the belles-lettres be motivated by a thirst for vituperation? It casts not light but the darkness of mere exasperation into literature. If you like that sort of thing, it is the sort of thing you will like, as the old drama critics used to say. And yet, lest one carry an "ethical silence" so far it is quite misunderstood, perhaps it is permissible to identify it. One does not refrain from blasting the bad boys of Crane studies because of cowardice or incapacity or because they are invulnerable. On the contrary, one refrains by conviction, in the faith that the useful study of literature is not conducted in such a spirit.

As I was taught the theory of that part of historiography which is the critical examination of what purport to be historical documents, its rules begin in the old motto of the Roman market: "Caveat emptor"—"Let the buyer beware." I never had a colleague who, from the ground of his long, danger-filled years of Crane study and collecting, more insistently reinforced that lesson than Lester Wells. Practically, everything I have learned about Crane documentation echoes again, "Caveat!" It seems to hold true for examples of every variety of what presents itself as evidence: whether textual, documentary, or journalistic, even of memorabilia or ana. In Crane's case not very much even of holograph documentation can stand unchallengeably alone. Writing a letter, he could not be relied upon to get the date, day of the week, month, or even year right. Was he christened with, or did he seriously assume, a middle name or initial? Probably not, at least not really; but what evidence exists which bears on the point appears to be scrambled. It has all made life extraordinarily difficult for editors and biographers.

A fascinating example appeared among the files carefully a-massed by Lester Wells. This was the typescript, with old snapshots pasted in, of a volume called "Stephen Crane: A Personal Record," by perhaps the most reliable of Crane's New York artist friends, Corwin Knapp Linson, nowadays, say art dealers, a collectible painter. Written during the 1920s, it proved unpublishable at the time, and Linson had sold it, together with other memorabilia, to

Wells for Syracuse University. To read Linson's manuscript was to find nugget after nugget of information and insight regarding his famous friend.

What Linson had written, however, was not a book. He had no idea of building intellectual or thematic structure into a memoir, and his treasure was a bag of loose rocks. Only a Maxwell Perkins could have led Linson through the agony of working his materials into a book. On the other hand, it seemed clear that the manuscript could be salvaged for scholarship by thinking out a design "to concentrate and clarify Linson's narrative while preserving it as his story, registered through his personality, and speaking his words with his voice," as the editor's introduction says.[2]

Upon enquiry from Wells, the aged Linson responded that he would be happy to see his book edited and published. However, I turned to the manuscript with a word of caution from Lester Wells, who had learned to know Linson, as he knew other survivors among Crane's acquaintance, shrewdly. Linson, approaching the age of ninety, naturally thought otherwise from the Bohemian, New York - style, he had been when, at about age thirty, he knew Crane. No doubt he had thought still differently when, about age sixty, he first worked on the manuscript. He had made later efforts to revise. For one thing, Linson justly felt indignant about the nonsensical legends connecting Crane to the conventional myth of Romantic Satanism. For another, somewhere along the line Linson had become a firm, conservative Lutheran. The editor had to be wary of distorting effects from that conversion.

Such, together with judgments stemming from what was known about Crane as a preacher's kid, an explorer of American low-life, an athlete, a military school boy and a fraternity man, a journalist and an associate of Bohemians—his "Indians"—provided the motive for a decision in editing the book that Crane could not have gone around saying, prissily, "The hair-oil he does!" I made him, and pointedly recorded the change, say, "The hell he does!"

Wells reported after publication that Linson's one objection to the book as edited rose from that assault upon his accuracy. Now I think he could have been right and I wrong. For the shock value—"You mustn't say the naughty word," as a Victorian joke-song put it—Crane could have gone around at the famous Pike County camp-out, for instance, drawling, "The hair-oil he does!" Also, it might be guessed at reasonably good odds that, in reaction to the sulphurous conversation of his artistic and medical student

"Indians," Crane had studied delivering that phrase as a well-timed, campy put-on.

Score one for Linson? But there is another case in point. Some of Linson's photographs were unique, of the highest biographical importance. They had bent, buckled, cracked, faded, and yellowed with time, being sixty years old and having spent about half of that time pasted on pages of typing paper. Easily the most precious showed Crane posed on Linson's studio couch beside the collection of *Century* magazines from which Linson recorded Crane's reading the serial publication of *Battles and Leaders of the Civil War* while preparing *The Red Badge of Courage*. The shot serves as the frontispiece (without acknowledgment of its restorer) to *The Third Violet* in the *Virginia Edition*. As it stood on Linson's page, that most important picture was in the worst condition of all. Lester Wells mournfully thought it unpublishable, irrecoverable. He consented gladly to any effort at salvage.

Though I did not know either whether the photos could be recovered, I was lucky to have a great photographer for a generous friend. I mentioned the problem to Jack Lunn Mowers, and he said, "Bring them over to my darkroom some evening, and we'll see." I am too ignorant of the processes even to describe what went on as he put those wrecks through bath after bath, print after print, playing magically with light and shadow; but we ended up with solid, glossy, unquestionably publishable copies.

Then my friend surprised me. "If I know anything about the business," he said of a photo which claimed to present Crane as he looked after writing "The Pace of Youth" all one night, "this one has been drastically retouched. Let me print it up as it stands so the University can lose nothing, and then let's see what happens when we try to clean it."

What happened as he cleaned it, presumably of paint, unfolded a drama of darkroom historiographical criticism. The bowl disappeared from Crane's pipe, the suggestion of a pen in his hand elongated to unite with his pipe-stem. Behind the tube began to appear bottles, looking more and more like brandy. Out of the darkness emerged the face and part of a figure belonging to a man dressed in the same strange costume as Crane. Now we could glimpse a reasonable explanation for the odd clothing and for the original posture and hand-position too awkward for an author who had labored all night and was still at work. Not writing but smoking the then popular hookah, not alone but at a party, Crane had been photographed (rigidly still for an interior night-shot by flash-powder) at a shindig put on by "Indians" costumed in working medical-school attire for the occasion.

Perceptibly neither drunk nor spaced out on a drug, Crane looks clear-eyed and controlled, the tension of long posing registered in the sinews of his hands. Why did Linson the old painter fake the picture? Perhaps Lester Wells's insights into the man explain.

Lunn Mowers's triumph in rectifying a document, a Crane source, raised shocking questions. Could one trust anything Linson said, now? Should we scrap the project? How does one decide? We concluded that one decides by looking to the probabilities, the run of the odds, testing everything in Linson against what we knew about him as witness and about the subject generally. Wells had many years of experience with the study of Crane, had often been compelled to judge among reliable, more or less probable, and spurious Craneana, from anecdotes and baseballs to documents and pyrography; I was already working through an often uncharted wilderness of materials for the first of Howells biographies. We had ready access to outside historiographical expertise.

Should we publish the "before and after" pictures? The publisher decided not. It would, he feared, too much endanger a book he thought economically marginal at best. Linson might sue. The Press couldn't give us the space necessary to explain: "Too academic. It runs against the tone and feel of the book."

And that was why, remembering the best of American personal literary memoirs, we adapted the title from Howells's recollections of Mark Twain. We tried to set Linson's book on its own feet and called it, by editorial fiat, *My Stephen Crane*. It has stood up well for the quarter of a century during which Stephen Crane studies have developed from an arcanum into a scholarly field. I no more think the retouched photo will bring it down than what may have been my incapacity to distinguish between "hell" and "hair-oil."

Nevertheless, both matters illustrate the problem of the elusive Stephen Crane. He tempts interpreters, like me regarding "hair-oil," to hasty conclusions and thence, sometimes, to dubious unitary generalizations. And some of what masquerades as hard evidence about him tends to be more than ordinarily treacherous. There is ample reason to suspect that not one of the so-called eye-witness testimonies about Stephen Crane will withstand strict histor-iographical criticism. What Lillie Brandon may have told anybody—or what was written or said by Lucius Button or Willis

A. *Linson photo of Crane, entitled "Vignette—when writing 'The Pace of Youth'." Print restoration by Jack Lunn Mowers.*

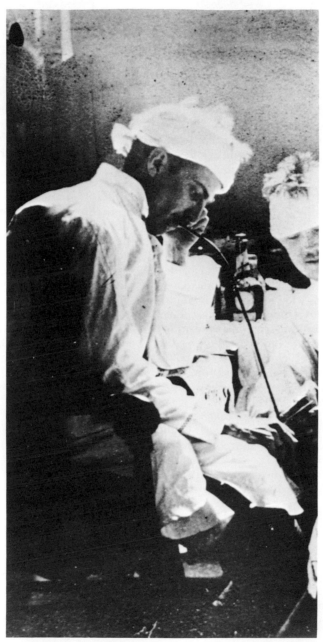

B.   Photo A after cleaning by Jack Lunn Mowers to reveal original state.

Hawkins or Frederic Lawrence or Frank Noxon or anybody else who "knew Stephen Crane when"—is shaky. Not to mention the special problems of Cora Crane or the legendary perjuries of McCumber or Becker, I think my favorite impossibility came from Mansfield French, who played baseball with Crane at Syracuse. To the end of his long and I believe admirable life, French insisted that during Crane's semester at Syracuse he sang in the choir of the local Episcopal church every Sunday. All other evidence about Crane's religious ideas and sentiments argues against French, of course.

For reasons just about as strong, I never believed that Crane wrote the first draft of *Maggie* in the Delta Upsilon house at Syracuse, either. No more did Wells, himself a D.U. I am sure it could be demonstrated by the stylometric methods of A. Q. Morton's *Literary Detection: How to Prove Authorship and Fraud in Literature and Documents*, 1978, that the author of what Crane was writing in 1891 could not have written *Maggie*, though I don't suppose one need go that far to demonstrate a rather obvious point. What credibility in Crane documentation comes down to is the same as what every historiographical or biographical problem comes down to. Under useful rules of evidence, the elements of proof must tend to flow into a mainstream of probability to which a reasonable, disinterested mind would give credence. Is that ever perfectly sure and safe? No, never. The point is that Crane's case incessantly presents peculiar difficulties. Documents and witnesses seem to be unusually skewed. It seems reasonable to suspect that Crane himself wanted to keep elusive.

Everybody knows that, in effect as a profession, the press in his time was out to get Crane. Crane knew it, and the contents of the scrapbook in the Barrett Collection at Virginia of items gathered for him by a clipping-service bear him out. Some journalists maliciously and systematically lied. He must have been good copy, stirring wide, immediate reader interest. Among the newspaper funny-men, the paragraphers, it became a national game to see who could think up the most outrageous jibe at Stephen Crane, whether they knew him or not. But there was a personal factor, not easy to explain, in the equation, too. The old Fourth Estate hated his guts. I remember vividly how the face of Samuel Hopkins Adams flushed and his eye flashed, though he was a civilized man past ninety, when he recounted how his colleagues on the *Sun,* and all real reporters, despised Crane. More than half a century after Stephen Crane's death, Adams still hated him, personally: he was "undisciplined, irresponsible." All that too, of course, skews evidence.

In short, "the New York Kid," one of Crane's literary masks, remains what the author painted him—a hard-luck kid. Even within the Crane industry too few of its captains seem to like him very much; and it remains rather a cottage industry because its workers tend to remain amateurs. The Crane industry has not been rationalized, certainly not pacified. More war is to come.

Nowhere have those facts become more glaring than with regard to what should be the definitive foundation for solid Crane studies—the monumental *Virginia Edition of The Works of Stephen Crane*. Officially the textual work has been done by Fredson Bowers, who edits everybody, with his infallible yet unstable dogmatics of textual procedure. The *Edition* does, for all practical purposes, I believe, gather the texts of Stephen Crane on one shelf. No one need now range from Hanover, N.H., to Syracuse and New York City, to San Marino, Calif., and thence to Charlottesville just to read him. Though small occasional pieces, new holographs, and perhaps a few unrecovered newspaper writings may pop to the surface, I do not think they are apt to change our perceptions radically.

Neither ought one to minimize the achievements of Bowers and his staff in registering a great complex of potential knowledge for the Crane scholar or critic. One of the as yet far too little recognized contributions of every CEAA or CSE edition is its necessarily massive presentation of evidence regarding the sources and family tree of each text: the histories of composition, printings, and textual variants—authorized or corrupt—from the beginnings through the last contact of the author with his text. In the mass of all the editions together, that evidence, when it is recognized by scholars, will alter American literary history as, from each separate edition, it tends to alter the biography of the author. There is much in the textual apparatus of the *Virginia Edition* to educate the Crane scholar. And the serious, not to say furious, challenges being raised against it may produce dividends in further knowledge yet.

Two examples will have to suffice to illustrate the troubles of the *Virginia Edition*; but they concern two of Crane's most important texts, those of *Maggie, a Girl of the Streets* and *The Red Badge of Courage*. Millions of dollars and many years of strenuous human living have been bet nationwide (against unsettling argument and authority, by the way) in support of Fredson Bowers's theory of copy-text and the necessity for conservative treatment of it. In editing *Maggie*, Bowers decided, against the majority faith among

editors, the CEAA Manual, and, in effect, against ruling national
opinion established by acceptance of the force of his arguments and
authority, to break his own rules. He altered a decisive moment
within the 1893 edition which he chose as the basis for his text to
conform it to the admittedly corrupt 1896 text. His argument in
self-defense looked to critical, esthetic judgments of the work and to
an enormous decision to go behind all evidence to a personal
assurance that he alone understood the inward, creative, esthetic
mind of the author. In the realms of esthetics and creative psychology, to say nothing of Crane studies, Professor Bowers, however
learned an expert in general textual bibliography, is an amateur.
Like Donald Pizer, Joseph Katz, and Hershel Parker[3] (and almost
everybody else), I thought Bowers was wrong. As an original
member of the CEAA Board and the quondam general editor of a
major edition, I felt betrayed.

On the case of *The Red Badge of Courage* and its text, the jury is
not even out yet. The adversary process is in full swing. Emotions
tend to be heated by a condition in the *Red Badge* volume of the
Virginia Edition somewhat reminiscent of the *Maggie* problem. The
Red Badge volume contains 516 pages. Of these, 132 present the
clear text of *The Red Badge of Courage*. The ratio runs almost three
to one against the novel. The remaining 384 pages are devoted to
twelve pages of front matter and seventy-nine pages of a critical introduction by Professor J. C. Levenson. That leaves the textual
editor a snug 193 pages, roughly 150 percent of the length of
Crane's clear text, for his needs.

Professor Levenson's "Introduction" is of course competent
(everything he does is good). But I am not sure it is better, or even
quite so good, as the late William Charvat's pioneering "Introduction To *The Scarlet Letter*" in the Ohio State Centenary Edition of
Hawthorne. I have always thought Charvat's introduction the first
not only in time but quality, the template for literary editors' introductions to definitive editions. It occupies thirteen pages of well-
leaded type.

Meanwhile, back on the stricken bibliographical field, Bowers
and his hard-worked staff have two opponents—each of whom
would seem to have something to fear from the other. The one
seems to be a platoon led by Professor Hershel Parker, also textual
editor of the Melville Edition, who, in a sense being more orthodox
than the Pope, more royalist than the king, have found Bowers's
text replete with error according to Bowers and have returned,

perhaps puritanically, to the one true "conservative" copy-text, the Barrett manuscript. The third party is Professor Donald Pizer, who says of his new "Norton Critical Edition" that, in the light of Crane's long, hard effort to revise and revise and get it right, "we should permit Crane the last word—that of the Appleton text . . . the 1895 edition, conservatively emended" for "obvious errors."

Professor Henry Binder, interestingly, has prepared a third text for the newly revised *Norton Anthology of American Literature.* Binder would allow Crane little ground for legitimate rewriting and arrives at a very chthonic *Red Badge* indeed. In a sense the situation is one Crane might have enjoyed: "Which Norton text d'ya read?" But there is a taste of the tears of things in it, too. The original motive on which all that treasure and life was poured out for CEAA was that we were to have editions as nearly exact and permanent as the state of the art in our times would permit. The last question of a Cranean irony obtrudes: shall we ever, after all? Most if not all these issues, with a number of others, are discussed in the "Special Number on Stephen Crane," *Studies in the Novel* (Spring 1978), edited by Parker (for discussion of which see "Selected Bibliography" with which this volume concludes).

In part what much of the foregoing illustrates is that Crane easily eludes the fireworks of professorial bad temper, which is seldom really concerned about him anyhow. The situation also suggests that the scholarly frontier is biographical. Getting at the facts and getting them straight remains the challenge. If from the latest biography one were to separate out the conjectural or uncritically credited allegations of fact, and then dispense with the stretches of literary criticism, there would be left no very impressive residue of biographical novelty.

In Crane biography generally there is too much fiction disguised as flat fact, too much assertion not clearly distinguishable from fiction. Whether or not Crane was an impressionist, Beer, Berryman, and Stallman were. When it came to a choice, therefore, all three biographers opted for the "artistic" before the evidentiary. Perhaps the major difference was that Berryman, at least, really was a poet. In short, the biographies, like too much of the rest of the Crane corpus, leave a reader with more unanswerable questions than one can handle. "How does he know that?" asks the reader; but deponent saith not. The sources, again, do not serve. Some have not been put on record. The late Miss Lillian Gilkes, coeditor of the standard Crane *Letters,* felt free to be frankly indignant about some of the relationships of printed texts to sources. The "definitive" text, again, has become a field of battle. Collectors are said to be sitting on key documents. Somewhere, the elusive Stephen Crane laughs ironically.

No little, I suspect, of the scandal of evidence relating to him may be traceable at last to that same Crane's deliberate making. He meant to be, needed to be, elusive; and he has probably won. What are we to do? For one thing, give up "fox-hole" scholarship. The situation calls for pluralism; and perhaps we have let our metaphors get mixed. Sir Isaiah Berlin's distinction between sorts of minds—the "hedgehog" and the "fox"—may apply better to the point. Crane's was above all else the mind of the "fox"—mercurial, wide-ranging, easily giving us hounds the slip. Perhaps a Jamesian pluralism is fitting, and a Keatsian negative capability. It would be all right, then, for the blue-chip Crane scholar to be wrong just like the rest of us. But he would have to confront and accept his fallibility, too. Perhaps we all need to attend to what both Frost and Faulkner seem to have said to their biographers. Writers, living centrally in the imagination, having to care most for the power to create art, become professional liars. Even more than most folks, they lose track of the facts as the Recording Angel might be said to know them: "Don't trust a word I say."

CHAPTER 2

The Youthful Stranger

S TEPHEN,[1] born the first of November, 1871, was the ninth to
survive among the fourteen children of the Reverend Doctor
Jonathan Townley Crane and Mary Helen Peck Crane. He was thus
the late, last darling of a big family, the babe of his parents' age;
and he was both blest and doomed to the life of what the
denominational colleges branded "a PK"—a Preacher's Kid. Dr.
Crane, as presiding elder (what would now be called District
Superintendent) of the Newark, New Jersey, district of the
Methodist Episcopal Church, was a beloved and weighty servant.
He had labored for his Lord as preacher, teacher, school and area
administrator, writer, and pastor. Success had corrupted neither his
sacrificial spirit, his admired sense of humor, nor the gentleness of
his thought and feelings. His brilliant boy, no doubt mistakenly,
would later suppose him to have been simply innocent of evil. As
Christian, scholar, and gentleman, Jonathan Crane is more likely
merely to have thought evil overrated.

Stephen's mother naturally made an excellent parsonage wife.
She was the daughter and sister of a redoubtable tribe of upstate
New York Methodist preachers. The Pecks had moved from the
years of back-woods exhorting to those of booming industrialism
without much altering their camp-meeting tough mindedness or
their minatory language. They took evil with puritanical seriousness.

Dr. Crane, however, had become a Methodist in rebellion against
the fierceness of his Presbyterian heritage and defiance of a
Princeton education. It was in the spirit of Horace Bushnell, not of
Peter Cartwright, that he wrote his books. To promote love,
redemption, and Christian nurture, he had warned against the
dangers of *Popular Amusements* (1869) and *Arts of Intoxication*
(1870). But the core of his thought he expressed in *Holiness the
Birthright of all God's Children* (1874). It was, as Daniel Hoffman

has shown, rather against the essentially vulgar damnation-evangel of the Pecks than against his father's thought that Stephen would revolt.

The essence of Stephen Crane's situation was that he must revolt. The laconic penetration of collegiate wit produced the brand "PK" as a sufficient explanation for eccentric, defiant behavior. Was some classmate, attractive and gifted, running wild? Oh, just another "PK." After eighteen years of genteel poverty, of tyranny from the Official Board, the Ladies' Aid, and the Eye of the Community, of parental meekness toward the tyrants and suppression if not oppression of the child; after ten or a dozen moves, each into somebody else's house in a new town with an unknown and therefore less predictable set of tyrants; after a lifetime of newness in eight or nine different schools, with the problems of the new children in his peer group intolerably intensified by his being the mysterious, sacrosanct, easily hated minister's child; after years of loneliness and repression, it was not to be wondered at that at college the liberated not infrequently broke into strange patterns of revolt in the effort to define and discover themselves. Even in narrow, unsophisticated denominational colleges people developed wisdom and tolerance in forbearing with "PK's."

And theirs was, on the whole, the early fate of Stephen Crane. His father changed districts in 1872 and moved his family in 1874. He left administration for a pastorate in Paterson, New Jersey, and moved his home in 1876. He left the metropolitan area in 1878 to move to a final church in leafy Port Jervis at the hilly meeting point of New York, New Jersey, and Pennsylvania. That final move may have been out of care for the frail health of blond, spindly Stevie. And Stevie went to school for the first time in Port Jervis that September, almost seven years old, securely literate, and so furiously humiliated at being put with the first-graders that he jumped two grades in six weeks. With his peers in Port Jervis he experienced those militant intricacies of boyhood in a deceptively simple small town which were amply documented by Thomas Bailey Aldrich, Mark Twain, and W. D. Howells before they were reimaged by Stephen Crane, author of *The Whilomville Stories* (1900). But in Crane the after-nostalgia for "Whilom" was sharpened by the fact that his "happy childhood" in Port Jervis was intolerably brief. After some eighteen months of Dr. Crane's usual success in the new church, that tired saint suddenly died on February 16, 1880, and Stephen Crane became an orphan at seven.

I

Much of the amateur-Freudian speculation that this or that literary invention of Crane represents revolt against his father must face the fact that Stephen never knew his father well. With what images of father he grew up, we shall never know exactly. But there are items in Crane's heritage from that good man which can be reasonably evidenced. What Stephen was to make of his heritage is not yet to the point. Its content may be seen as, predictably, religious and moral concern, a care for personal cultivation and expression, and, perhaps less expectedly, certain ideals of aristocracy. All of these conspired to intensify the isolation from common experience already sprung from the social situation of the preacher's kid.

That none of the other eight surviving Crane children became particularly distinguished is a little surprising. Protestant ministers have contributed gifted children to the world out of all genetic ratio to their numbers. Perhaps Stephen's was a case of the superiority of a child of his parents' age. Melvin Schoberlin tells us that Stephen's nearest sibling, Agnes, was a school teacher who early promoted his reading and herself yearned to be an author. Little came of that, as of other family ambitions.

Yet nothing seems to deny that the family circle was warm nor that Jonathan and Mary Helen Crane's piety illuminated their home. Hoffman persuades one that his father's religion of love, of the inner voice and light, remained the positive base of Stephen's profoundest and nakedest metaphysical statements, those made in his poetry. Of course the father's death shocked young Stevie and left him resentful (why should anyone have been startled to find that out?). Afterward he passed through a youthful period of innocent piety; then adolescent revolt set in and he simply stopped discussing theology with a mother who argued like "a wave" for Peck ideas less humane and intelligent than Dr. Crane's. At the end of the ends, however, the point is that Stephen's religious heritage set certain focal requirements upon his vision. He couldn't *not* employ the engaged moral concern, the expectation of love, the demand for sacrifice, and the exaltation of real innocence (which Jonathan Townley Crane's religion enforced) as check points against what he thought he saw occurring in the worlds within and without.

The family care for cultivation and expression did not in itself make Stephen Crane a great writer. But it seems safe to say that he might not have turned author unless he had grown up among books and with people who habitually expressed themselves well. There is Beer's oft-repeated story of the towhead looking up seriously from his papers on the floor to ask, "Ma, how do you spell 'O'?" Upon application, one much-gifted graduate "PK" explained the plethora of talent in the type by saying, in effect: "We never had a house of our own. We never had good things to sleep on or eat off. People gave us all sorts of ugly things, and we had to take them. But we did have books. All the good young people came to our house to talk. We cared for ideas and such art as we knew and cared terribly."

Certainly the known facts about the Crane family concern for cultivation go far toward explaining the mystery of Stephen's artistic mastery in the face of his weak formal education. He learned the essential thing—how to use books to his purpose—without, if not in spite of, his colleges. It is arguable that he was better off with his quality of self-education than any academic program could have made him. At least that was what his contemporary Robert Frost discovered in his own case.

"The new baby is a boy and we have named him Stephen for his ancestor who signed the Declaration," wrote Dr. Crane the morning after his last son's birth. If the ancestor did not actually sign the Declaration of Independence, he might have. Himself descended from an original Stephen who had settled Elisabethtown, New Jersey, in 1665 and founded a family of local gentry, that ancestor served his nascent state and republic with distinction and lost two sons (including another Stephen) in the Revolution. The writer—famous, young and with a reputation for irreverence to keep—would tell the *Newark Sunday Call* that the Cranes had been "pretty hot people" and made him "about as much of a Jerseyman as you can find." Even as he wrote that in 1896, he must have been aware that industrial megalopolis and trailing suburbia were making Old Jersey one with Tyre. Obviously, what had been a small gentry, a local aristocracy, ceased to matter when their towns and country disappeared.

Yet the sense of something fine was concealed under the flippancy of "pretty hot people." Dr. Crane had been conspicuous for gentlemanliness among his professional colleagues. Sister Agnes is known to have aspired to be a Christian lady. And it is demonstrably clear that Stephen would to the end of his days cherish his own version of the great American ideal of the Christian gentleman.

To make Christian gentlemen of American youth was throughout most of the history of the Republic a major declared aim of American secondary and higher education. In the colleges it was one of the comparatively few points at which the abyss between the student half of "college life" and the official "educational" half of the community could be bridged. The voluntary associations—the "societies" and the fraternities with their mottoes and rituals—on which "college life" was founded emphasized the pattern of ideas and its value components sharply. That held true not only for WASP but for Catholic religious training: preaching, teaching, church literature (from the Sunday School "paper" to the Reverend Mr. Crane's and other preachers' books), and churchly organizations were shot through with the ideal of the Christian gentleman.

Precollege organizations—the Christian Endeavor, the Epworth League, De Molay—extracollegiate organizations—the YMCA—also hammered at American transformation of the ideal. The Catholic Church, in direct line from the synthesis of the ideal from its pagan heroic, its chivalric, and its monastic origins, taught it, apparently, as seemed appropriate to a given parish, though certain implications of the existence of the Knights of Columbus seem obvious.

All this is to say that, especially for a "PK," a student at Pennington, Claverack, and Syracuse, a Delta Upsilon, knowledge of the ideal had been larded into Stephen Crane. Now, what one finds revolting and what one must continually and consciously revolt against, he cannot help taking seriously. As is said of atheists—there are two kinds, those who do not believe in God and those who hate God—so Crane felt about both "Christianity as it may be seen around town" and "the society man," a fake gentleman. He hated them passionately and strove to transcend them. His condition compares to another bit of folk-say, "Christianity would be the finest religion in the world if anybody ever tried it."

About Crane's personal qualities of gentlemanliness, Joseph Conrad (and who was a better witness?) is almost breathtaking. As Conrad testified in his introduction to Beer's biography, he saw in his friend Stephen "the delicacy of sentiment, of the inborn fineness of nature" which he "had managed to preserve like a sacred heritage. . . . one could depend on it on all occasions. . . . He was all through of the same material, incapable of affectation. . . ."

And again, "Though the word is discredited now and may sound
pretentious, I will say that there was in Crane a strain of chivalry
which made him safe to trust with one's life. To be recognizably a
man of honour carries no limitations against human weaknesses, but
comports more rigid limitations in personal relations . . . these
restraints which are inherent in the character of a man of honour,
however weak or luckless he may be."[2]

Again, Conrad speaking of Crane, "As to his humanity . . . it
was a shining thing without a flaw." And, last, "His was an un-
restrainedly generous temperament." Anyone who thinks that
Crane himself lacked Conrad's perceptions needs look no further
than his letters to Nellie Crouse, though the evidences appear in
many places.

One could make a long list of the constituent concepts and values
obviously treasured by the artistic imagination of Stephen Crane
and by Crane the man which conform to the ideal. Did he himself
sometimes sin against them? Yes, and he said so and abased himself
for it. Not exclusively, of course, those are both Christian and
gentlemanly acts. Not untypically of his times (or ours) Crane
valued the ideal and its components in defiance of society and social
hypocrisies, especially the loud mouthings and public, Pharisaical
demonstrations of credence. But his art set forth and he tried,
sometimes quixotically, sometimes effectively, to make it existen-
tially real. I do not think he or his art can be understood unless one
perceives that—among many other things.[3]

II

If that concept always would be part of the story of Stephen
Crane's inner weather, there was to be a long history of outer
happening before he grew up. After her husband's death, Mrs.
Crane fluttered to a boardinghouse near Paterson where Stevie
promptly suffered scarlet fever. Then she took him back to Port Jervis where a second cycle of Whilomville days lasted until May 1883.
Then at the age of eleven, he was taken to complete much of his
boyhood education in the fatefully appropriate town of Asbury
Park, New Jersey.

Naming it for Francis Asbury, the great circuit-riding true
founder of their church in America, the Methodists had established
a resort on the beaches of southern New Jersey. Connecting directly
to the south was the rigidly controlled conference center of Ocean

Grove, and just below that the Chautauqua-type cultural center of Avon-by-the-Sea. There Mrs. Crane was drawn, apparently by the prospect of summer employment as a speaker to Methodist women's groups. Her son Townley had a reasonably successful news agency, and the family was reorganized about as well as might have been hoped after the father's death. At Asbury Park, Stephen was at least somewhat free of the burdens of the preacher's kid, and the location held wonderful potentialities for education in the world of the American *fin de siècle*.

Its setting, of course, presented—the thundering surf on the white sand beach, the ships and ocean weather—materials to absorb which would some day place Crane among the great writers of the sea. But the human phenomena the setting attracted around him also taught Stephen severe lessons in plural standards of morality. To that rural isolation of sea, sand, and empty back country were drawn crowds of visitors parading wealth, vulgarity or sophistication, and self-indulgent leisure. Naturally there was the tension normal in resort towns between natives and tourists, exploiters and exploited, hustlers and suckers. To have any glimpse from the inside of the processes thus involved makes for cynicism; and Crane was by temperament, by childhood training as a preacher's kid, and by the nature of his own slightly detached situation in the town, supremely an observer. But the discrepancies of appearance and reality in Asbury Park were redoubled by its official, ecclesiastical status. It was hard to keep Asbury Park from becoming just a fun town accentuating the difference between saints and sinners, Methodists and worldlings. Its resident founder and czar had to fight against too much freedom from wintertime conventions. Sex, both as prostitution and as vacation assignations, liquor, and gambling kept edging in. Young lovers found a sordid sanctuary under the boardwalk.

Riding his pony over the beaches and back through the brush and eventually pursuing news items for Townley, Stephen Crane came to know the area intimately. Thomas Beer records the story that Stephen once saw a white girl stabbed by her black lover. He stayed away from prayer meetings (except when he gladdened his mother's heart by unexpectedly attending after being made tipsy by his first introduction to the red *vino* of a "nefarious Florentine"). He took up with the local sporting crowd, swiftly developing a passion for baseball (flouting his father's cautions against popular amusements). Sometime in this period his mother lost control over him. When he left Asbury Park for military school at the age of fifteen or sixteen, he was a confirmed smoker. Not only had Dr. Crane upon *Arts of Intoxication* been set at nought; Stephen was flying in the face of all Methodism, to say nothing of official Asbury Park.

III

Perhaps it is significant that Crane in after years went back to Port Jervis for "Whilom" friends rather than to Asbury Park. It was his fate never to have a hometown or even, in the sense of place, a home. Strong inner activity, especially reverie life and reading, must have compensated. The Asbury Park years—roughly his twelfth to seventeenth—would have been decisive in any life; in Crane's they were fateful. They confirmed in the sensitive, vulnerable, fatherless preacher's kid his fate as *isolato*. He learned to make outward, comradely terms with the world of men, but not with that of women, as an overtly masculine figure. He played games, especially baseball, with fiendish drive; he smoked and swore ostentatiously; he gloried in the appearance of what was evil to his elders. But careful observers noted that he lit cigarettes and let them burn to ashes in his stained fingers, that he slid a drink around on a bar and left it unconsumed.

Stephen Crane in the Asbury Park years became elaborately conformed to his present world in some of its obviously "un-Christian" ways. But actually he was *in* but not *of* it. Inwardly and truly he was an *isolato*, a stranger and a sojourner, a spy in the world. He was not, of course, therefore a Christian. He was admirably preparing to become an artist. *Isolato*-rebel, rebel-*isolato*—who could say which quite came first, though each condition bred the other? The immediate fact was that his mother had lost control of him, and she no doubt began to have open as well as intuitive evidence of the fact.

The time-honored solution was to send the boy away to school. Apparently Mrs. Crane first tried the Pennington Seminary of which Dr. Crane had been principal for ten years before the Civil War, and that parental surrogate failed. Next, according to L. U. Pratt, on January 4, 1888, Stephen arrived at the Hudson River Institute in Claverack, New York, with a rack of big pipes and a surface so tough he immediately moved into the leadership circle. It occurred to nobody to think him a parsonage sissy.

Actually, the two and a half years which took him from entrance to Claverack at seventeen to exit from Syracuse in June 1891, at nineteen, were all of a piece. They formed an essential middle of the education which began on the boardwalk at Asbury Park and finished among the Bowery bums and Bohemians of Old New York in about 1894, when he was twenty-two or twenty-three.

The institution Crane liked to call "old C.C." (because it had absorbed the moribund Claverack College) was a somewhat indeterminate institution—a military prep school with vestiges of a junior college. It gave Crane four very important things: military experience, academic training, the collegiate feeling, and athletic achievement. Ironically (as his entire preparation for life was to be ironic), it cheated him on all of its first three gifts. And no doubt he knew it. Its military character was make-believe. Its academic training was amateurish even by the feeble standards of the day. In an age when college life first became a glamorous public reality in the United States, Claverack could offer only an impoverished, distantly improvised imitation. Only the athletics were "real." College seemed as phony as Asbury Park.

What was confirmed therefore by his college was the baffling figure of Crane the floating, *déclassé* aristocrat. "Stevie is like the wind in Scripture," sighed Mrs. Crane. "He bloweth whither he listeth." "After all, I cannot help vanishing and disappearing and dissolving," wrote Crane at the height of success. "It is my foremost trait."[4]

As a type, the self-conscious *déclassé* is a figure more important to the genesis of American literature than has been realized. To name only some obvious authors, his characteristics have been shared by Freneau, Cooper, Poe, Emerson, Hawthorne, Melville, Henry James, and Scott Fitzgerald. Orphaned, impoverished, disinherited, clear superiority denied or disregarded, he often knew drear November in his soul. Communication with the world being impossible, he withdrew to mighty dreams and scornful observation of the herd. Alienation taught him an elusive, floating quality. And it inclined him to moods ambiguously self-pitying and ironic. In the keenest minds the irony became double-edged; it turned back upon the posturing self and bit deep.

It ought to go without saying that personal histories and temperaments made for wide individual variations of the type. But Crane was never to outlive his representative purity. Ford Madox Ford noticed in him "a great deal of the defiant mistrust that the French called *méfiance*," and a striking ability to play exasperating roles.[5] And we are lucky to have recorded from Claverack days the sensitive but maliciously cold-fish vision of Crane registered by a painter, Harvey Wickham.

Wickham was drilled in Company C of the student battalion by "1st Lieutenant" Crane and never forgave his officer's "perfectly hen-like attitude toward the rank and file." The implication is that Crane's ardor for drilling his company to victory in the yearly Review was not shared by Wickham and the Private discovered that "Stevie was not tender of other people's vanities." Wickham's unhappy eye saw that, though Crane went around "in a dirty old sweater," his chum was "the richest boy in school" and dressed "in the height of collegiate fashion." Wickham the esthete baited Crane into his choir in the village Methodist church with red-haired Harriet Mathison. "He had a light, pleasant voice, true in pitch, if of no very great power or compass," Wickham judged. He saw that, though Crane talked only of "poker and baseball" in a tone suggesting *"noblesse oblige,"* he had to tread softly with the authorities. He detected Crane's profound "fear of ridicule, especially of his own." And he concluded of Stevie that "all his life he strove to win recognition as a regular fellow . . . and he failed. Only women and hero worshippers ever really liked him [the exception was other artists, but warmed-over resentments barred the grown Wickham from the grown Crane]. He wanted to be a democrat and yet a dictator. Hence that contradiction, self-depreciation coupled with arrogance . . . his chum was the richest boy in school."

That damnable iteration about roommate Earl Reeves's money sufficiently betrays Wickham. His malice veiled the whole truth, but it revealed portions a kindlier eye might not have seen. The friendlier view would have noted the earnestness of the boy who went about drawling. "Ho, hell." He fell madly in love also with Jennie Pierce and made, as he later recalled, "a pure complete ass" of himself. He played baseball well enough to have to decline the captaincy of the team. He was gazetted Captain of Company C. It was "the happiest period of my life although I was not then aware of it," he wrote one of the Claverack co-eds all of six years later.[6] But even then he was *in,* not *of* it.

His *méfiance* was directed at the academic conventions of college life. Bawling stage-drivers and baggage-smashers in Arkansas, he wrote in 1895, were "as unintelligible as a row of Homeric experts."[7] But his portraits in *Active Service* of student high-jinks are as contemptuous as those of the heroine's professor-father. And when he went, presumably in response to maternal practicality, to study mining-engineering at Lafayette instead of returning to Claverack in 1890, he defined himself unforgettably in reaction against the conventions of student life.

Lafayette was very much "Old Siwash" in its attitudes. Crane started in acceptably by joining the Delta Upsilon fraternity. But the next week a band of hazing sophomores came to "get" him at his dormitory room. When he refused to open it, they broke down the door—and stopped. A later-arriving witness saw that "Steve was petrified with fear and stood in a grotesque nightgown in one corner of the room with a revolver in his hand. His usual sallow complexion seemed to be a ghastly green . . . both arms were limp and the revolver was pointed to the floor."[8] That might have been panic from the start. It might more likely have been Crane's shock proceeding from the realization that he had nearly murdered somebody in defense of his personal honor. Crane was hazed no more.

By Christmas, Stephen had flunked out of Lafayette; and a family council during the vacation apparently determined to enter him at Syracuse, which had been founded largely by his mother's uncle, the late Bishop Jesse Peck.

As soon as he could get out of the Widow Peck's house and into the Delta Upsilon lodge, Crane began to find Syracuse more *simpático* in ways not academic—"although the fellows here *are* somewhat slow," he confided back to "old C.C."[9] It was a "dandy house" in a "dandy city," and there were "some damn pretty girls" around. There were also enough Claverackians to make up an alumni association, of which Crane became secretary-treasurer, and some old chums from Port Jervis. Some of the slow Methodists forced him and other smokers into the chilly cupola so as not to have the house tainted by the fumes. But they accepted the deliberately scandalous Stevie, according him the notorious liberties of the "P. K."

The faculty tried letting him have his head as a special student; gave him an "A" in the only course he completed (English literature under Chancellor Charles N. Sims); let his first published tale appear in the *University Herald;* and made him permanently, if not immediately, grateful by trying tactfully to snatch his brand from the burning. The students let him star on a winning varsity baseball team; let him bully them a bit socially and bully-rag them a bit about police courts, journalism, and real life; and apparently enjoyed his iconoclasm. His nicotine-stained fingers and tough poses and his telling professors that he knew what St. Paul said but disagreed with him and, more cogently, that Miss Frances Willard, the sentimental reformer, was "a fool," no doubt set up mild shock-waves. But the Methodists appear, after their fashion, to have understood.

The College annual, *The Onondagan,* gaily listed Stephen Crane in a column headed "Grinds" and illustrated with a little garland of memorial verse:

> Sweet drop of pure and pearly light,
> In thee the rays of virtue shine,
> More calmly clear, more mildly bright
> Than any gem that gilds the mine.

The tribute was a memorial because Crane was gone. He would spend an important summer reporting Asbury Park news for his brother Townley and the *New York Tribune.* He would take an important camping trip with Port Jervis boys. But he left Syracuse with an understanding with one of them, Fred Lawrence, that they would not return. Next fall Lawrence would begin medical study in New York and Steve would go along and room with him: not for medical study, but, as the antique statement runs, to seek his fortune—perhaps journalism, perhaps literature, perhaps. . . .

His formal education was over.

IV

In the fall his real education decisively began in New York. It was to lead to a dark and complex knowledge of the life and nature of man; to an astonishing flowering in the command of an art (his datable writing thus far had been sophomoric); to stark privation of body and psyche through long and bitter discipline, agony, and defeat to breathtaking victory. And to the knowledge, final with Crane, that the priceless victory was prizeless and empty.

He began life in New York as he mostly continued in failure or success, stony broke. Perhaps nothing is so basic to an understanding of Stephen Crane's life as a clear grasp of how he handled money and of what that means. But to date there have come to light virtually no records. The impression one gets is that he lived by a Bohemian code—borrowing and cadging when he had no money, open-handed to others when he had. But there seems to be no way of proving anything about the subject.

The dates and sequences of many events in these crucial years are obscure. Apparently Stephen began to ease into New York by living with his brother Edmund in Lake View, New Jersey, within easy commuting distance. From there he could make forays to the city for job-hunting, for getting up studies for free-lance articles, for seeing people, and for studying the new life of man in polygot, industrial megalopolis. It was apparently all right at "Ed's house" if he disappeared for days at a time while staying with some friend who had a "place" in the city. W. D. Howells, who did not yet know Crane, would begin in March 1892, to publish chapters of a novel keenly prescient of Crane's situation: *The World of Chance.*

The great curse of Victorian Christianity was its inability to distinguish between humanity and respectability. The effects, bad enough in green Port Jervis and queer Asbury Park, were catastrophic in the cities. There the poor and outcast swarmed in their immigrant and proletarian millions. Like the cities, these people were phenomena of the industrialization of Western life which overwhelmed the culture with massive problems for which it had few and feeble solutions. Precisely because the churches had largely chosen to ignore these throngs and their problems, Stephen Crane, one guesses, chose to join those who were determined to confront, explore, and understand. Abjuring theology, he chose to take up the personal task, the same as a Christian (but not a "respectable") task, to understand.

While Crane was at Claverack, Howells had set the country tingling with *A Hazard of New Fortunes*, a novel which insisted that we not "forget" the poor, the agonized, the trapped in screaming megalopolis. It scarified with its ironies both those who would not remember and those who could not bring themselves to be compassionate with the poor as persons. It dramatized with power the situation of the rising number of those who were seeking to go down to the slums and help. Whatever his inspirations, Crane seems to have begun to go down himself from Piety Hill to the canal waterfront slums in Syracuse and to write of what he saw in streets, saloons, and police court.

But the ideal place was New York. Everything was bigger, intenser, and worse there. And worst of all was the Bowery. It was, Crane protested to Miss Helen Trent, an older beauty with whom he fell disastrously in love late in the summer of 1891, "the most interesting place in New York." And he was studying it so intimately he showed up one night with a shiner acquired when a stray beer bottle thrown in a saloon fight hit him in the eye. He was mastering the technique for studying people and places. He took advantage of protective coloration: "the youthful stranger with the blonde and innocent hair."[10] He was inconspicuous, silent but a good listener who encouraged talk, an expert stalker of his game. A wartime correspondent was fascinated afterwards to watch Crane's perfect technique. He could associate with thieves and cutthroats, even in foreign ports, and never be harmed. He sat "soaking in knowledge of the reactions of the kind of men he liked to write about . . . a sombre, silent member, contributing no adventure of his own, never flushing his quarry with a word that was not in their vocabulary."[11] He bagged his game.

Such expertise came slowly, of course. And its mastery, as well as its exercise in "human interest" vignettes of increasing literary but low news value, interfered with Crane's thrust toward professional journalism. He had worked as a "stringer" on papers since Claverack. A quite possible solution to the problem of a career—even one which might at length support literature—was newspaper work. In 1891 he was a valuable part of his brother Townley's news agency from Asbury Park, and he found a job as stringer on the *New York Tribune*. In August, caught in an absurd episode with Asbury correspondence for the *Tribune*, he got himself fired and Townley's agency ruined. Briefly in early 1892 he held but lost a job with the *Herald*. It became clear that he was to find no salaried "basis" for other writing in journalism.

The reasons for his lack of acceptance as a journalist are complex and a little obscure. Mere reporting—"Who-What-Where-When-How Much"—bored Crane. To "Why-How-How-it-Felt," he responded passionately. But that was for stars, not cubs. The rude disciplines of the chaotic offices disgusted him. His study and respond method, slowly mastered, eventually made him a superb feature writer. When studying a fire, a traffic jam, an epileptic down in the street, a drunk, a restaurant, Coney Island, the crowds and what they said and did, and the police who vaguely ruled them, Crane commanded his New York as few artists have ever done and as no one else before the Ashcan painters did. In an informal will which he wrote on the way to his "Open Boat" adventure in 1896, he said accurately to his brother William, "Some of my best work is contained in short things which I have written for various publications. . . . There are some fifteen or twenty short sketches of New York street life and so on which I intended to have published in book form under the title of 'Midnight Sketches.' That should be your first care." Midnight sketches were fine training for literature but not for reporting.

Another contributing factor to his lack of success as a journalist may have been that Crane simply didn't get along with reporters. His friends were the circle of old Claverack and Port Jervis chums and other artists—writers, painters, actors. To reporters he seemed aloof, "stuck up," arty, snooty, and spoiled. When opportunity offered, they would lay for him in the "paragraphs." One suspects that to him they seemed frantic and corrupt—and that they caught him studying them. At any rate, he was forced into a life of preparation for becoming an artist. He had all the time there was to learn to see with his own eyes and find the words to create the same vision in the mind of a reader. And he could rewrite, revise, and write again his story about a girl of the streets.

From a strictly artistic point of view, this almost pure apprenticeship might seem all to the good. Other things being equal, it was almost ideal. But there was one key factor wholly out of balance: money. With deliberate stoicism, Crane suffered bitter physical privation, through the winters, particularly, of 1892 - 1893 and 1893 - 1894. He was in no danger of "forgetting" the sufferings of the poor in the slums. He shared them to learn and practice his art and, in the pathetic, infuriating case of the 1893 *Maggie*, to publish it. He lived in virtual madhouse dormitories of medical students and artists. He sponged on strugglers only a little less impecunious for a bed, a meal, for a little warmth, quiet, and relative privacy in which to write. He wore his shoes to tatters for want of carfare and days came when he couldn't go out because he could no longer patch the holes with paper—he was literally "on his uppers." Parts of *The Red Badge of Courage* he wrote "on the paper the meat came home in."[12] He went ill-clad and cold. Penniless, he actually starved at times, and he was malnourished for much of three years.

Some of his deprivation resulted from pride. When he came to the point of collapse, there was always a Linson, a Vosburgh, a Gordon, a Garland to bail him out. He was welcome at his brothers' houses and retreated to Ed's at Lake View and later Hartwood, New York, or to Will's at Port Jervis. But how often can a self-respecting man be bailed out? How often, how much can he borrow? How

long can be practice his art and admit it will not feed him? No
doubt some of Crane's agony proceeded from improvidence. And
yet—was it really improvidence to risk all on printing *Maggie*?
What's provident? Can the life of an artist truly be so in an acquisitive culture? Financially shrewd Howells thought not. Modern
nations are finding ways to subvent their artists and starve no more
Cranes.

Whether pride or art or character caused it, Crane's suffering was
real; and it produced important effects. It ruined his teeth, wracked
his body, and doubtless presented him the tuberculosis which eventually killed him. It affected his psyche and imagination profound-
ly. If nothing else, it confirmed emphatically his intellectual and
perhaps temperamentally necessary conviction that the condition of
human life is war.

V

Bitterly losing many skirmishes and some battles, Crane sorely
but steadily won through to victory in his combined struggles to
become a recognized artist and deserve it. Given the circumstances,
it is surprising that he persevered, wonderful that he won out,
astonishing that he succeeded so early, and simply unaccountable
that his level of achievement was so high. There is no better definition of genius. One famous abstract way of defining genius is the
"capacity for taking infinite pains" or "application of the seat of the
pants to the seat of the chair" way of describing the thrust of powerful energies. Crane had capacity to endure, but his ability to lift his
art from the nonentity of his writing at Syracuse through the mixed
qualities of the *Sullivan County Sketches* and "Midnight Sketches"
to the achieved but various styles of *Maggie, The Black Riders*, and
The Red Badge of Courage concretizes the definition.

But a better definition of genius is that it does prodigiously what
others do feebly or not at all. Crane produced all this brilliance
between his twentieth and twenty-fifth years. This accomplishment
made him another "marvelous boy," an incredible prentice.
Howells found himself remembering the myth of the birth of
Minerva in remarking that Crane had sprung into life fully armed.

Strictly speaking, however, Howells knew better. He knew what a
price Crane had paid. His contact through Garland with Crane
became one of the fateful inspirations of Crane's life. It began distantly when Crane heard Garland lecture at Avon-by-the-Sea in

1891 about his friend and master, Howells. Crane reported it so well for the *Tribune* that Garland looked him up. They became good enough friends for Crane to be emboldened to present Garland with a copy of the privately printed *Maggie* when Garland returned to New York. Garland, who knew Howells would like it, made Crane send him a copy. When he read it, Howells, who made a life-habit of sponsoring the young, not only liked it immensely but had Crane to tea and listened to him all evening. He began to scheme to get *Maggie* regularly published and also began to read Crane's manuscripts, to see that editor's doors opened for him, to publicize him as judiciously as he could.

Howells was the reigning Dean of American letters. His critical arm was the longest and strongest in the nation. No one he sponsored as a brilliant young man remained unknown. His endorsement was the one most courted and angled after. To Crane it came through merit (and the agony of printing *Maggie*) and with it came Howells's warm friendship. Crane testified repeatedly to the warmth of his response. Garland and Howells seem to have nerved, even in part inspired, him to the achievement of the 1893 - 95 period which made him great.

Even with Howells's help, Crane continued to be jinxed. Not all the Dean's personal intervention would persuade booksellers to push *Maggie;* and even B. O. Flower, the reform editor, somehow failed to republish it, though Garland reviewed it in Flower's *Arena.* Crane sold nothing in 1893. But he had the courage and encouragement to go on. He wrote short stories about the doomed baby, Tommie, from *Maggie.* He and a painter friend, Corwin Knapp Linson, tried collaborating on an illustrated version of Crane's humor, "The Reluctant Voyagers," and Linson was thrilled to pick Steve up one morning and find him wearily concluding an all-night sitting which produced "The Pace of Youth." Still nothing would sell.

In desperation Crane thought of turning out a pot-boiler—a historical romance about the Civil War. He began to do research in, among other places, Linson's studio, where copies of the *Century Magazine's* "Battles and Leaders of the Civil War" lay handy to the divan and there was shelter out of the cold, spring rains of New York and quiet while Linson worked. But it was clear almost from the beginning that Crane was incapable of mere lucrative swashbucklering. In the midst of Linson's silent sketching one day, Crane, "squatting like an Indian among the magazines," blew up: "I wonder that *some* of these fellows don't tell how they *felt* in

those scraps! They spout eternally of what they *did*, but they are as
emotionless as rocks!" He would need to work his imagination
through the whole spectrum of "how they *felt*" before he would
know why they did not talk about emotion. When he had done so,
The Red Badge of Courage would be very popular. It would also be
the work of a serious artist, not a hack.

Nobody knows how many versions Crane wrote of *The Red
Badge*. One could document seven "states" of the manuscript from
surviving pages, but obviously much went before. Linson says that a
first draft was done in March 1893, and "the full manuscript" completed at Lake View the following summer. Whether that second
draft is the one which survives fragmentarily on the verso of its
successor nobody knows. When Crane came back to town in the fall
wearing rubber boots because his shoes were gone, he had a
treasure in manuscript form. But he was several times on the point
of collapse before fortune shifted.

Until it did, however, he moved, as a kind of ward of a bunch of
"Indians" of young artists, into the old Art Students' League
Building. There, perhaps because hearing Howells read the poetry
of the newly discovered Emily Dickinson unlocked fresh creative
impulses,[13] Crane began suddenly to write poetry in defiance of the
yowling jeers of the "Indians." Of course it was not like Dickinson's; her revolution had only unleashed his. His was more *outré:*

> In the desert
> I saw a creature, naked, bestial,
> Who, squatting upon the ground,
> Held his heart in his hands,
> And ate of it.
> I said, "Is it good, friend?"
> "It is bitter,—bitter," he answered;
> "But I like it
> Because it is bitter,
> And because it is my heart."

The imagery was often surrealistic as well as dramatic, and the
"lining"—the special gift of knowing just where to begin and end a
line—had an artistry equalled only by the greatest masters of *vers
libre.*

Crane brought his poems to Linson, who was struck dumb by the
procession of pictures trouping across his inner eye. He came with
them to Garland, who was incredulous—and then so flabbergasted,

when he discovered that Crane had a packet of the "pills" in his head and could and did sit down and write one out without pause, that he began to wonder if the right explanation were not spiritualism. Crane, however, was no "medium"; he was just a starved, almost desperate genius. [14] He was speaking out his deepest intimations about life in art as original as art becomes.

And still there were troubles. Not even Howells could persuade Alden of *Harper's,* an editor with whom he had worked closely for years, to buy a few poems. The *Arena* bought a tale and a sketch; the *New York Press* began to take Crane "specials," trumpeting their catch with a glorious interview-tribute from Howells; McClure began a promising but exasperating flirtation. John D. Barry of *Forum* volunteered to read Crane's *Lines* before the "Uncut Leaves Society" when the poet said he'd "rather die than do it" and shuddered privately while a quartet of old comrades went to see how "Lord Fauntleroy's mother" would take it. By April Crane had moved to a flat and of an evening could go with Linson and the other semi-employed for seventy-five-cent French dinners with something that passed for wine. Eating, he told Garland, was "charming." He began to negotiate with a publisher about his poems, and he had long since recovered *The Red Badge* from its "hock" to the typist (whether he ever repaid those from whom he borrowed the sum of his pawn or not).

His basic education was done. He had acquired unique literary skills, and he exercised them with a mastery acknowledged by coveted acclaim. He could now expect to feed himself. If he could keep his wells of creative impulse flowing and control the personal life his bitter experience had discovered, he could hope for a major literary career. The best judges told him so.

VI

There were to be, of course, difficulties to come. Of his life since childhood, the summer of 1894 was perhaps the most light hearted and appropriate for twenty-three-year-old Stephen Crane. He had another slum novelette, *George's Mother,* to write and *The Red Badge* to polish. Linson and he did an article about a Scranton, Pennsylvania, coal mine for *McClure's,* which was business, fun, and enlightenment all together. In Port Jervis, Crane played for hilarious hours with Will's children and renewed his feel for "Whilomville" at an instant when his imagination was most sensitized. His sympathies for children under the tyrannies of convention were reawakened, too. When at the end of summer he was in Albany, he took a couple of little boys trapped in their mamas' adoration of Little Lord Fauntleroy's curls out and paid for their haircuts—never mind what mama would say.

And that was just after a rollicking time when, instead of the old August roughing-it group of four Port Jervis boys out in Sullivan County, New York, a couple of dozen "bob-cats" of both sexes (meticulously chaperoned) went camping in Pike County, Pennsylvania. They boated, swam, hiked, and ate standing at a long rough table "like the animals we were," Linson recalled. "In the orange light of a great campfire we gathered of evenings and perched on low branches and logs, Stephen with his back to a tree picking at a guitar." All in the out of doors they played games, flirted, and laughed—and sang, but above all, they laughed. The sportsman Crane, muscular, sanguine, identifying mystically with beautiful nature—the Crane so often forgotten and lost in the other Crane—had full play. The life was innocent, healthy, and gay.

When it was done, Crane and Louis Senger guffawed all through a night getting out a mock-newspaper, the *Pike County Puzzle*, to commemorate the occasion. Everybody got roasted brown, and especially "S. C." There was, for example, a note of enquiry:

What can I do with my voice? Stephen Crane.
In the spring, Stephen, you can plough with it, but after corn ripens you will have to seek employment in the blue-stone works. We have seen voices like yours used effectively for cider presses.

Perhaps that good time gave him courage to be adamant in refusing to let Copeland and Day push all the defiant religion out of the poems in *The Black Riders*. S. S. McClure kept *The Red Badge* for six months, neither finally taking it nor letting it go until Crane, justifiably, almost cracked up about it. Finally he took the manuscript away and "sold" it to Irving Bacheller's infant syndicate—sold 18,000 words of it, that is, for half a cent a word: $90. But at least it was a breakthrough, for real fame and a certain kind of fortune followed. The syndicate story ran in the *Philadelphia Press*, December 3 to 8, and in the *New York Press* all on Sunday, December 9—and, according to Berryman, in something like 750 small papers around the country. Crane heard from California about the story before Christmas, and the *Press* chain began to puff its author most flatteringly. Bacheller wanted to send him West as a roving correspondent at once, but Crane delayed—to have Christmas "at home" and to read proof on *The Black Riders*. He hung around New York through most of January, negotiating with publishers in Boston about the poems and in New York about *The Red Badge*. He got the former well settled and interested Ripley Hitchcock of Appleton's in the latter. By January 30, 1895, he was in St. Louis, poised on the threshold of the West.

A hundred years before Crane, narratives of Indian captivities designed to be uplifting accumulated prosperity for ironic reasons: they let readers by civilized firesides feel themselves part of a wilderness experience distant enough to be romantic. Then Cooper painted Hawkeye and Chingachgook. And whole cycles of the American imagination began to turn about the matter of the West. There was every reason why Stephen Crane should have known all sorts of literary Wests—in novels both serious and "dime," in the tales of strayed cowboys he had variously befriended, in the *Police Gazette*, and especially in the great magazines to which he himself aspired and in which Remington and Roosevelt and Owen Wister ruled the roost. The West was romance, wilderness, primitive simplicity, and sport—the testing of muscle, nerve, and manliness; above all, it was adventure. And wonderfully enough, Crane, the observer trained to silent nonparticipation, experienced a fascinating number of adventures. Some were like romances, some like the Bowery, some like Remington-Roosevelt-Wister, and some could have happened only to Stephen Crane.

His first adventure was better keyed to Garland's *Main-Travelled Roads* than to Wister. From St. Louis he plunged into drought and then blizzard-blasted Dawson County, Nebraska, to report on the "Nebraskans' Bitter Fight for Life." With all the graphic power of his color and simile-laden style, he drummed up aid for the farmers brave under "the strange and unspeakable punishment of nature." He bespoke sympathy for the ill-organized Relief Commissions "involved in a mighty tangle" of "enormous difficulties" and staggering under a torment of abuse from "thugs" and self-righteous "philanthropists"—whom Crane equated. He recorded equally the plights of the abandoned horses drifting before the winds, who could not speak, and of the people eating the horses' feed who could:

"I hain't had no aid."
"How do you get along?"
"Don't git along, stranger. Who the hell told you I did get along?" [15]

It made good copy for Bacheller, but it put Crane in a self-examining mood. He talked bitterly to red-haired young Willa Cather in the *Lincoln State Journal* office, and he was moved perhaps also by the fact that she was the first woman to whom he could really talk about his life and art. He had to lead a double life—reporter and artist, he said. Literature cost him infinite time and pain to filter it through his blood, to drag it out of his "hidebound" imagination. In the same mood and place he wrote Clarence Peaslee about the centrality of labor and honesty in art.

And perhaps the next night Crane learned something about the ethos of the West. Stepping between a big man and a little man punching each other in a bar fight, he was astonished to be collared by a cursing mob and dragged—for disturbing the peace—before a justice who let him off on the grounds of ignorance. It seems the two fought every night, and it was taken for granted. Crane's intended gallantry was a public nuisance. It was a story he might have invented.

En route to New Orleans he stopped over to write of the "sporting" life among "The Merry Throng at Hot Springs," Arkansas. In New Orleans he revised *The Red Badge* one last time and sent the proofs back to Appleton's for publication. Then he headed for the land of the cowboy. There seem to have been quick touristy forays off the trains into Arizona and Nevada. Somewhere he heard the Apache scalp-dance and somewhere he acquired huge, silver spurs and "a large Smith and Wesson revolver" to match. He was well prepared for the adventure which met him on the Alamo Plaza in San Antonio in March.

There the "haunting solicitude" which a Syracuse fraternity brother remembered in Crane was wakened by sounds of sobbing from the curbstone. Edward Grover, sixteen and a runaway from Chicago with sixty dollars in birthday money to become a cowboy, was broke; rejected even by the Army, he had come to the end of his rope. Crane fed him and poured out the last of his own cash to put him on a train and to wire the boy's family. What matter that Crane would be thrown out of his hotel? It was a lot warmer than New York. His later note to Grover was perfect in its tone: "Dear Deadeye Dick: Thanks for sending back my money so fast. The

hotel trun me out as my friends of the Bowery say and I was living
in the Mex diggings with a pack of sheep men till my boss in New
York wired me money. Now, old man, take some advice from a
tough jay from back East . . . stay home and grow a mustache
before you rush out into the red universe any more."

Then Crane took off into Mexico, and it was perfect. The mountain grandeur stirred his ingrained *Naturmystik*. The strange
language and new culture sharpened his perceptions, deepened his
sense of wonder, opened windows upon self-realization—provided
him all the joys of the traveler. "Mexican Sights and Street Scenes,"
as he wrote them up for Bacheller, gave him to ironies about the
suffering of burros, birds, and people in a gently callous, a calmly
cruel society. The raffish international set in Mexico City was a joy.
But the key adventure was altogether the real thing.

The principal record of this sojourn is the fine tale,
"Horses—One Dash." There is no way, from what one knows of
Crane's normal tendency to refocus events into literature, to tell
what "really" happened. He went out with a local guide into the
territory of Ramon Colorado, a small *bandido;* perhaps he went to
interview a bandit for Bacheller, or to see what he could see, and
Colorado found him first. The skeleton of the tale is that, when
Crane and his guide took lodging in a sinister hamlet, a drunken,
swaggering bandit and crew came in; and, just the other side of the
doorway, they sat feasting, swilling, and bragging up their courage
to burst in and rob the Americano of his money, revolver, and spurs.
Crane knew the deepest physical fear of his personal life to date and
the guide gibbered; but, just as the bandits seemed about to burst
in, a bevy of local whores arrived and diverted them. Crane and the
guide then sneaked out at daybreak and rode madly ahead of
Colorado and crew until saved by a patrol of *rurales*. These events
are the gist of the tale as he wrote it—and apparently as he told it
with gusto before he wrote it.

The despatches to Bacheller were meanwhile keeping his
memory alive at home. They appeared not as news but as features
and often long after Crane had left Mexico. The *Philadelphia Press*
on May 19, 1895, subheaded "Mexican Sights and Street Scenes" as
"The Author of 'The Red Badge of Courage' in the Aztec Capital."
And on July 21, "Ancient Capital of Montezuma / The Brilliant
Author of 'The Black Riders' Describes a Trip." *The Black Riders*
was announced for publication on May 11, 1895. It may have been
that event, the climax of what was probably the happiest twelve-

month's span in his life, which brought Crane back home in May.[16]

VII

Fame, praise, and deference could be more dangerous than neglect and abuse, Crane was shortly to find, but not yet. The advent of *The Black Riders* discovered a fascinating fact about his fame: his contemporaries couldn't bear it, especially the newspaper boys. Serious criticism, which mostly came along in the fall, treated his revolution seriously. But the "paragraphers," paid to be clever, howled like the "Indians" in Vosburgh's studio. Crane seems to have understood their envy, their need to feel outraged and reach for corrective satire, the commercialism which inspired their cracks and epithets, and their scores of usually stupid parodies. "I was the mark for every humorist in the country," he remarked later—but he survived to write more verse. "Abuse and ridicule" hurt a man of dignity; but they were insignificant beside the allegiance of "men of sense": Garland, Howells, and in this case, also Harry Thurston Peck, Barry, the reviewer for the *Nation*, and even the *Atlantic Monthly*.[17]

Crane discovered shortly that a group of lesser "men of sense" around Bacheller not only thought him clubable but wished to make him the star of the Lantern Club, sometimes called in the *fin de siècle* mode "The Lanthorne." It was a shanty on a rooftop approachable only by an iron ladder. There was lunch every day, and Howells and Mark Twain each came. On Saturday nights stories were read on assignment, and nothing but dispraise was allowed. "The highest tribute that a story could receive was complete silence," Bacheller recalled. Not only close friends like Edward Marshall and Willis Hawkins belonged but also Richard Watson Gilder, who had found *Maggie* too tough for the *Century Magazine*.

Crane's summer was another good one, including a renewal of the grand Pike County picnic. He rode, hiked, and hunted out of Ed's new home in lovely Hartwood, New York. He began to write up Mexico, and started a novel about the Art Students' League Building "Indians" which became *The Third Violet*. And then the long-sought fame descended.

At first it did not look like nemesis. Appleton's published *The Red Badge of Courage* early in October 1895, and the reviews were good in spite of a few cavils in New York. Crane began to get interested letters from editors as well as fans. Elbert Hubbard of the *Philistine* got up an elaborate testimonial dinner for the "cause" of Crane (and the greater glory of Fra Elbertus), and Willis Hawkins persuaded Steve to go—even supplying the dinner jacket and overcoat. And Crane had one moment of sheer, joyous triumph. As he wrote to Hawkins:

> The dinner scheme mingles my emotions. In one sense, it portends an Ordeal but in the larger sense it overwhelms me in pride and arrogance to think that I have such friends.
>
> By the way, you ought to see the effect of such things on my family. Ain't they swelled up, though! Gee! I simply can't go around and see 'em near enough. It's great. I am no longer a black sheep but a star.[18]

Obviously, even in this whoop of joy Crane's feelings were mingled. He had every reason to fear deflation, if from nothing else than self-ridicule. Life was still full of obstacles. He took his catboat out into the lake and sent it booming through a new part where sunken stumps, snags, and old logs gave it thump after shuddering thump. With each his anger rose till, all alone, he flew into screaming hysteria—the first time in his life he had ever completely lost his temper, he told Hawkins.

Perhaps that was therapeutic. The Philistine dinner, in Buffalo, New York, was attended not by celebrities but by old friends and newspaper people—more "Indians." They acted that way, but there is no evidence that Crane was upset. Frank W. Noxon, an old D.U., thought Crane was "having the time of his life" amid the uproar, and Crane told Miss Nellie Crouse as much when he used a documented account of the affair as bait to open a correspondence with her on New Year's Eve;[19] his object, possibly, was matrimony.

CHAPTER 3

The Apprentice Sorcerer

ACTUALLY, of course, within four and a half years from
New Year's Day, 1896, Crane would be on his deathbed in the
Black Forest. 1896 might have become the year in which success
stabilized his personal life and his professional career and set him on
the way of growth which could have matured his genius and con-
ceivably set his achievement on the highest level. Instead, while the
books and fame piled up, Crane's life moved from one disaster to
another until by New Year's Day, 1897, he was, symbolically as well
as actually, aboard the filibuster tug *Commodore* off the coast of
Florida—sinking. He would burn out the year as he did his brief life
in restless, desperate seeking—for the right woman, the right way of
life, endurable relations with celebrity; for truth, control of his art,
command of his creative impulses—for something (who really
knows what?) hidden away in his psyche. As Howells remarked,
Crane sought "the secret of himself." He would remain a brilliant
apprentice to life and art.

Pretty obviously, no artist is "arrived" until he has mastered the
problems of his materials, the way of treating them, and the reasons
for treating them that way which will, altogether, permit his art. His
creative impulses must be quickened and freed to bring to light the
potentialities his technical skill can triumphantly convert. He may
have successively and repeatedly to master such problems as he
changes styles. But he must at least begin by serving whatever apprenticeship is necessary to his mastery. He must work, learn,
produce, imitate, discard, struggle, and bore into the secret of
himself.

In another but allied sense, the same is true of being young and
growing up. And of course young artists go through both processes
more or less at once. A few of them, as they experiment, produce
learner's work, "studio pieces," so brilliant as to constitute art

strangely true, even great. Perhaps that applies to all the poetry of Milton through "Lycidas." And certainly it applies to the best of Stephen Crane. He never lived into the exact secret of himself. And no more shall we. The knowable secret of Stephen Crane is that in art, in life, in thought, he remained an experimenter, a Seeker, of rare, wonderful gifts, an apprentice sorcerer.

That it seems is the key to the interminable debates about whether Crane was realist, romanticist, neo-realist, naturalist, symbolist, impressionist, or what have you. He was any kind of an "—ist" available to him from the weather of his times because he was investigating, experimenting with it all and trying to find out which best suited him. But he was not any of them, really, because he had no time to settle on any. He did an astonishing amount of brilliant work in various styles, from various viewpoints. He overpowered all by the force of his own imagination's way. But he did not live, unlike his contemporary Joyce, for instance, to establish what that way was.

In spite of Hubbard's Philistines and all, Crane seems to have taken the first hubbub over *The Red Badge* pretty well. He had begun it as a pot-boiler, and he knew Howells thought *Maggie* and *George's Mother* better. He was sure he could improve on them all. He was habituated to "abuse" over *The Black Riders* and inclined to discount extremists. And then the wave of British adoration of *The Red Badge* swept in and smashed him right off his feet. The pressures of what critics were saying in London and of the reactions of people he knew threw Crane into something like panic.

The wave from abroad broke with the publication on January 26, 1896, of a dispatch to the *New York Times* by its London correspondent, the American novelist Harold Frederic: "Stephen Crane's Triumph"—the kind of story every young writer dreams of meriting. The praise was unstinting for Crane's "unique grasp" of subject and his originality of "construction." Frederic guessed perceptively that the author had imagined, not participated in, war. Frederic understood *The Red Badge of Courage* more fully than any other reviewer and called it "one of the deathless books which must be read by everybody who desires to be, or to seem, a connoisseur of fiction." He proclaimed that literary London rang with the name of Stephen Crane.

In dealing with Crane, one is forced to guess. And one good guess seems to be that word of Frederic's piece got around literary New

York a few days before the Sunday *Times* printed it. At the Lantern
Club, horse-play ceased while a solemn toast was drunk to
Crane—and what he called "the social crisis" hit him. He could
only "call them damned fools and sit down again."[1] In New York he
became "a gibbering idiot," as he wrote Ripley Hitchcock.[2]
". . . Oh you don't know how that damned city tore my heart out
by the roots and flung it under the heels of its noise," he apologized
to Hawkins. ". . . On Friday it had me keyed to a point where I
was no more than a wild beast and I had to make a dash willy-
nilly."[3] He fled to the hills of Hartwood. Thence, on the day
Frederic's piece would appear, he wrote Nellie Crouse and the next
day Howells of a moving, almost tragic fear that success and praise
would corrupt, delude, or swerve him from the paths of truth,
honor, and courage. In a life always to be young, it was a moment
of rare and profound self-penetration.

Such self-knowledge might help, as it did, with the morale of
Crane's situation. It did not help with the key career problem—where to go from here? In a year's time his position as writer
had been reversed. *The Black Riders* and *The Red Badge of
Courage* had been published. This year *George's Mother* would
appear. *Maggie* would be for the first time published (not merely
printed). McClure would bring out *The Little Regiment* in his
magazine and Appleton publish it between covers. Hubbard would
do the tiny *A Souvenir and a Medley*, and *The Third Violet* would
begin serialization. Crane was now in hot demand with syndicate
and magazine editors as well as publishers.

But all this writing came from his past. There remained the
young writer's terrible problem of what to write about next. Added
was the agony following first success: how to follow it up and keep
the career running. Crane's sense of life as a battle became now a
series of interlocking challenges to fights he was on the whole to
lose. His problems were: how to manage his success; how to find
the materials for a rise from rather than a mere continuation of that
challenged and potentially evanescent fame; more fundamentally,
how to secure that vision, that method, that art-style which was also
a life-style to see him through as theirs had the masters of the past.

I

Nothing came of going to Washington for McClure. And nothing
but real trouble came from trying to hark back to the "Midnight

Sketches" idea and muckrake the police of New York. Not even friendship with Police Commissioner Theodore Roosevelt saved Crane from a debacle. Apparently it had not occurred to Crane, used in his heart to obscurity, that he was ripe to be framed. But he was. His fame rested largely on sensation: what was to the Victorian American mind the blasphemy of *The Black Riders*, the febrile garishness of his style, the dirtiness of *Maggie: A Girl of the Streets*, the grimy pessimism of *George's Mother*, the Bohemianism of *The Third Violet*.

The century-long tradition of romantic reputation founded luridly on Byron, DeQuincey, Poe, seemed to apply perfectly to Stephen Crane. And there was no dearth of volunteers to plaster it on him. Thomas Beer calls his chapter on this period "Fame and Prejudice." Wholly false gossip about Crane's drunkenness and opium addiction were assiduously spread; and then, of course, since he had neither home nor wife and was a notorious Bowery haunter, women (Byron's vice). Obviously, to the Victorian mind, the author of *Maggie* must have been addicted to whores. Obviously also, in the tradition he was vulnerable to seduction stories. Semiprofessional Crane-baiters had New York ringing with such tales in 1896.[4]

And at least on the question of women, Crane handed them devastating ammunition. It is, in fact, impossible to know how much fire there was beneath the smoke. Much of the testimony of witnesses who could have known about Crane is contradictory. The surviving evidence lends itself to ambiguity of interpretation. One reads it one way if he commits himself to the faith that Crane was "guilty"—of promiscuity, of commercial vice. He reads it another if he decides that Crane was quixotic about women as about many things. Beer—like Crane's friends Linson, Noxon, and Gordon—was convinced of Crane's essential "innocence." Stallman, Gilkes, Zara and Katz, like Crane's friend Hilliard, are convinced of his "guilt." Berryman, who is accepted by Hoffman, has a lay-Freudian notion of Crane as a special case.

Everybody might agree, however, that the question remains complicated by the life-long preacher's kid's defiance of moralism—the *méfiance* which made him exult in the appearance of evil. Not only did he refuse to protect his reputation, he deliberately, publicly courted as a celebrity about New York the disapprobation he had been trained to avoid at all costs in childhood and had rebelliously sought since early adolescence in Asbury Park. Finally, as his defeated courtship of Miss Nellie Crouse of Akron, Ohio, suggests,

Crane in his twenty-fifth year showed signs of matrimonial inclina-
tion. It does not seem to have struck him that women, especially of
a certain age, might feel the same about him. The net result was
some kind of "involvement" with four disturbed, if not dis-
reputable, women in 1896.

The fourth of these eventually became "Mrs. Stephen Crane,"
but there is no evidence to convince a judicious observer that Crane
was either in love with any of the other three, or in bed with any of
them. The first was, according to Beer, Doris Watts of various
aliases. Crane let her touch him for various loans, and she seems to
have tried to blackmail him, perhaps into marriage. When Crane
finally came to call her off, she hurled a knife from her "Turkish
Corner" which nearly impaled him. The story reverberated around
New York.

Then came Dora Clark in a case one might guess that Crane
deliberately manufactured. Perhaps not, but some of the facts
tempt one to such an interpretation. Crane had been avowedly
studying the massively corrupt New York police. He had been in
touch with Theodore Roosevelt, the new commissioner whose clean-
up program the "Force" was energetically resisting. He sat on the
bench with Magistrate Brown of the Jefferson Market Court all day
on September 16, 1896. That night he sat in the Broadway Garden
with a couple of chorus girls until they were joined by Dora
Clark—who knew one of the girls but not Crane. Dora, twenty and
pretty, was not an ordinary girl-about-town. She had a recent, very
active police record, having been picked up on sight by plainclothes
men "half a dozen times in five weeks." She believed herself—and
reporters for the *Times* and *World*, at least, reflected her belief—to
be the victim of organized police persecution for having turned the
laugh on a detective in court, with a racial slur.

Was it accident that Crane was introduced to her? Or that he
took all three girls out on the corner and left Dora Clark talking to
one girl while he put the third on a street car—all in sight of a
plainclothes man whom Dora Clark apparently knew was standing
across the street? The policeman, Becker, much later electrocuted
for an extortion-murder, arrested Dora Clark for soliciting and tried
to run Crane and the other girl out of the picture by threats. When
it didn't work, he took them all to the station. The other girl, unfortunately for Crane, went into howling hysterics. Dora Clark was
locked up. The police sergeant tried to talk Crane out of wrecking
his reputation by appearing in the case. Next day the New York

papers carried flash accounts of Stephen Crane's appearance before Magistrate Brown to save a persecuted girl from a false charge of soliciting.

The news reports were, contrary to tradition, uniformly admiring of Crane, antipolice, and pro-Dora. The least factual and most fiction-like (though devoid of the obvious tags of his style) appeared in the *Journal* and was written by Crane himself.[5] It is by no means impossible that Crane, the reporters, and the girls had set a trap designed to protect Dora Clark, to expose and so help reform the police, and to pay short-run journalistic and long-run literary dividends to the writers. Whether that is so or not, the affair became a disaster.

In spite of newspaper protection, the affair spattered pitch on Crane that wouldn't come off. As late as the next January, papers in New England, Rochester, even Nashville jeered at the Crane whom the New York papers and the syndicates made a hero after the *Commodore* sinking. "The owners of the 'Commodore' as well as Dora Clark, must come to the conclusion that Stephen Crane is a Jonah," said the *Rochester Herald* on January 7. And the *Boston Advertiser* concurred on the ninth: "Novelist Crane is now in a position to tell us which he regards as the most dangerous way to get material for a realistic romance, seeing the elephant in the Tenderloin or enlisting on a filibustering Cuban expedition."[6] They represented others. Theodore Roosevelt and, for instance, Lincoln Steffens did nothing.

In spite of public promises from magistrates, the New York police no more stopped persecuting Dora Clark than they reformed for Roosevelt. They simply put Stephen Crane on the harassment list. And that may have made him seem the more vulnerable to a middle-aged, widowed, ex-actress, Amy Leslie, who worked as drama critic for the *Chicago News*. She had been an admirer of Crane and later claimed to have loaned him (or given him for deposit) $800. The facts are obscure. Crane gave Hawkins money for her, and for a long time he remained solicitous of her mental balance and was careful to remit money until she quarreled with Hawkins and eventually sued Crane. The *Chicago News* became one of the most flagrant and persistent of Crane-haters.

II

Whether or not Crane's New York affairs represented lust in action, they certainly cost a waste of spirit and an expense of shame.

They were disastrous to Crane's personal life and frustrating to his imagination. He got no literature out of any of them, except perhaps hints toward the absurd *femme fatale* of *Active Service*. He was little in advance of his condition at Claverack while reporting Harvard football games during that fall, 1896. But actually his situation was less desperate—or, from another point of view, more so—than it seemed. What should have been the normal context of New York had become chaos, development wholly blocked. He was waiting around town for orders "to ship" on a cloak-and-dagger filibustering expedition which he would report from rebellion-torn Cuba. He would see war at first hand.

Sometime in November he got his contract, put $700 in Bacheller's gold in a moneybelt, and took off for Jacksonville on the next train, too suddenly to tell anybody. There was journalistic logic in that for Bacheller; there was perhaps artistic as well as adventurous logic for the elusive Crane (who had just turned twenty-five). It has been suspected that there was a deep, hidden logic in it for a psyche looking for death—but who can really say? For the physical Crane the situation presently settled into ordinary military logic: he had hurried, now he waited.

While he waited, he met the climactic one of 1896's strange ladies. And, *pace* Berryman, she was very little like the others—or like anyone else he had ever known, except that she was a gallant, out-and-out rebel like himself. Cora Howorth Murphy Stewart, alias Taylor, had come a long and battered way from her mildly esthetic, prosperous, and certainly respectable Boston family. The informed conjectures of her biographer, Miss Lillian Gilkes, a tireless researcher, show Cora revolting against Boston; marrying and divorcing Murphy in New York; marrying Captain Donald Stewart, a much decorated soldier of Victoria's Empire, in London; leaving Stewart when he set forth upon overseas colonial service; and arriving at last (perhaps dumped from a junketing millionaire's yacht, who knows?) in Jacksonville. There she had gone into business on the "nice" edge of the underworld. She was mistress of the "Hotel de Dream," a nightclub with a local "class-A rating" as one "of the better houses of ill-fame."[7]

If, as Miss Gilkes argues, Cora was "technically" not a madam because her girls did not actually live there, hers was certainly at best a house of assignation and Mrs. Taylor was making a capitalist's success from the conduct of a "disorderly house." But there is no evidence that that was what especially attracted Stephen

Crane. He had a long wait in Jacksonville, and it was there Charles Michelson observed Crane's skill in stalking sailors and wharf-rats in waterfront dives. What with the publication of *Maggie* and his strange experiences with women and gossip, he may also have decided to "see" prostitution as he had hoped to see war. He later presented a different, full-fledged madam "on the line" an autographed copy of *Maggie*.[8]

But not even that would explain his fascination with Cora Taylor. In all his rather feeble writing about women, it seems clear that their Victorian games of irrational emotionality alternating with rigid convention simply suffocated Crane. It was one thing he never began to see through. In Cora, however, he found a woman of taste, intelligence, vitality, some good looks, who was incapable of playing the hypocritical games of respectability on him. It was not only that she was strategically misplaced for that; she was also intellectually and spiritually in revolt against it; and she conducted her person and her life with the integrity of courageous choice, as Miss Gilkes makes clear. Conventionally she was a lady *manquée* as Crane was a gentleman *manqué*. Of course it must have seemed, as serious love always seems, a matter of destiny when Cora fell frankly in love with him as he came to the "Hotel de Dream" while going "down the line."

Parenthetically, it may be useful to comment that Cora was not merely personally "aloof," like madams generally, from the main business conducted in her house. She was operating a "class" establishment; and her sophistication, poise, and charm provided the class. These characteristics surely were essential conditions for Crane's interest in her. Vice versa, it is difficult to suppose that, had Crane simply come rollicking through, paying his money and having his girl, Cora would have been smitten by him. Much more likely, he intrigued her in his natural role of the searcher into life for art.

The erstwhile preacher's kid, the temperamental (and now professional) watcher and self-watcher, must early have been roused to irony deeper than usual by the discovery that Captain Stewart was not only alive but vindictive: he would grant no divorce. It did not help with any of Crane's problems to discover that he could perhaps never regularly marry Cora. In the light of his reputation, what would become of them both if they were linked publicly? No expression of his love for Cora is happy, and the most lyric sounds like a farewell: "To C.P.S. / Love comes like the tall swift shadow

of a ship at night. . . . Then silence and a bitter silence—the
silence of the sea at night."[9]

III

Meanwhile there was the business for which he was carrying
Bacheller's gold-pieces and upon which he staked still more
precious hopes for his career. The business of filibustering (in this
case sneaking munitions to the Cuban rebels), consisted largely, as a
reporter colleague of Crane's recalled, in lurking. Dark, foggy con-
spiring wasted the weeks until at length on New Year's Day, 1897,
the tug *Commodore* got her guns and ammunition stowed and left,
amid rebel songs and muttered Spanish threats, for a little
beachhead. At once there were hints of disorganization and
sabotage. Water flooded the engine room the second night for no
apparent reason, the pumps failed, and she sank about dawn of
January 2.

The event was dangerous, exhausting, painful, shocking, but not
heroic. Experience once more dealt Crane bathos and disillusion for
his hopes. As might have been expected, there was chaos on the
sinking *Commodore* and things got worse at the end. Signed aboard
as able seaman at $20 per month as an official blind, Crane worked
himself almost to collapse bailing in the hellish engine room and
straining to get boats launched. Off himself in the last and littlest
one—a ten-foot dinghy with four or possibly five men in it—he had
to watch the drowning of the seven-man crew of the first mate's
boat which apparently foundered at the ship's side. Possibly what
happened was the drowning of three and the desertion of four
others on a raft after the ship sank—or possibly the raft was sucked
down by the drowning *Commodore.*

Then came the trip—of ten, twelve, fifteen, twenty miles (the
distance is in dispute)—across more or less dangerous waves (the
degree is in dispute).[10] It was a long, slow affair, perhaps much too-
long delayed by the crippled, mournful captain, who decided to lie
offshore all night rather than go in at dusk. When exhausted they
did go in, Billy Higgins, the oiler, the best man in the boat, was
meaninglessly killed in the surf.

Largely because Crane was in it, the *Commodore*'s filibuster had
aspects of a publicity circus from the start. On the day she sailed,
the New York *Press,* part of Bacheller's syndicate, not only announced it but listed essential items of cargo: 200,000 rifle car-

tridges, 1,000 Hotchkiss rounds, 2,000 dynamite cartridges, 1,000 pounds of dynamite, and "Stephen Crane, the novelist." On January 3, the *Press* screamed "Filibuster Sunk . . . Stephen Crane Missing," and word of his death flashed round the world. Next day the headlines read: "More of the Filibusters Safe / Commodore's Wrecked Seamen Struggle for Life in a Heavy Surf / Stephen Crane, Novelist, Swims Ashore / Young New York Writer Astonishes the Sea Dogs by His Courage in the Face of Death." The cook was quoted as saying not only that the "newspaper feller was a nervey man" but that Crane had rescued a fifth seaman from the dinghy (one never mentioned by Crane) and had himself been rescued by broken-armed Captain Murphy. It was not until January 7 that the *Press* had "Stephen Crane's Own Story."

In his "own story" Crane presented himself only as observer and Murphy and Higgins as heroes. His report said almost nothing about the hours in the dinghy. It is usual and probably correct to suppose that he held off because his imagination was already germinating its one true gain from all that agony. "The Open Boat," written in Jacksonville during the next couple of months, is one of the triumphs of Crane's creativity. It is one of the great tales of the period he was now fatally entering—which produced some of the world's great short stories but negligible novels.

The incident of the shipwreck is forever important because "The Open Boat" grew from it. But it was important also that the experience was deeply frustrating to Crane. He was loyal to Captain Murphy. And, yet, there were those seven marooned on and by the *Commodore:* in the first mate's plunge to death Crane had seen "rage, rage, rage unspeakable. . . ." And there was the loss of Billy Higgins. Had Murphy been treacherous, weak, mistaken, or merely trapped by mischance?

Crane never openly speculated. With Bacheller's gold probably at the bottom of the sea, Crane staggered "home" to Cora's frantic arms. He scraped together what money he could and slogged for weeks through Florida swamps trying to elude a *Commodore*-embarrassed United States Navy and failing. His family always thought his health was permanently wrecked in Florida. Defeated and more desperate than ever, he gave up in March and negotiated a contract with William Randolph Hearst to report on the incipient Greco-Turkish War. He began to announce that he had to see if *The Red Badge* really was right about war. Before he left Jacksonville it was apparently arranged that Cora Taylor would sell out and follow him to London and on to Greece, there to become "Imogene Carter," first woman war correspondent. He talked to Linson in New York about how to arrange a marriage without subjecting his affianced to the "weasels" of gossip. Then he sailed, never to "live" in the United States again.

IV

Nor is it clear that in any full sense he lived anywhere. Henceforth it was much a matter of conscious life in death, of a surviving which could not be long, must often be painful and only seldom, in his work, significant.

There was to be much too much building up to awful letdowns. In London he tasted his fame as only Londoners and Americans there knew how to serve it up to a visiting lion. Harold Frederic squired him around, and Richard Harding Davis took him into the brotherhood by giving a luncheon to meet J. M. Barrie, Justin McCarthy, and Anthony Hope. Heineman the publisher loaded him with compliments and got him a contract to write correspondence for the *Westminster Gazette*. Going down to Dover, Frederic and Crane were joined by Davis, a fabulous all-American-boy type. On the docks Davis saw "Lady Stewart" with Crane and, according to Miss Gilkes, recognized Cora Taylor of the "Hotel de Dream"—and froze.

Nevertheless Crane and "Imogene Carter" with her long-time companion, Mrs. Ruedy, went on to the war, touristing as they went. The war, when they got there, was a fiasco. Crane started out pro-Greek and optimistic about what "these people of the mountains" would do in their "people's war." But the war declared on April 17 ended in Greek humiliation by May 20, and Crane had only a brief chance to view combat (at a distance) with tragic exultation and to bleed psychically for refugees and betrayed soldiers. He got off at least thirteen dispatches,[11] however, including two which were among his best writing. They match Hemingway at his own game. Hearst's *Journal* headlined them flamboyantly: "That Was the Romance, 'The Red Badge of Courage'—a Story. This Is the Reality, a Battle Today in Greece—a Fact. By Stephen Crane"; and "My Talk With Soldiers Six."

He came out feeling that *The Red Badge* was all right. He did not see much in this war which his imagination had not told him, though his best writing about it is peculiarly conscious of variant possibilities in point of view. For he wrote:

The roll of musketry fire was tremendous. In the distance it sounded like the tearing of a cloth. Nearer it sounded like rain on a resonant roofing, and close by it was just long crash after crash. It was a beautiful sound; beautiful as had never been dreamed. It was more impressive than the roar of Niagara and finer than thunder or an avalanche, because it had the wonder of human tragedy in it. It was the most beautiful sound of my experience, barring no symphony. The crash of it was ideal.

This is from one point of view. The other might be taken from the men who died there. The slaughter of Turks was great, . . . the insane and almost wicked squadrons were practically annihilated, and their scattered fragments slid slowly back, leaving the plain black with wounded and dead men and horses.

From a distance it was like a game. No blood, no expressions of horror were to be seen; there were simply the movements of tiny doll tragedy.[12]

Or again:

. . . And this quality provided the picture with its extraordinary mysticism. These little black things streaming from here and there on the plain, what were they? What moved them to this? The power and majesty of this approach was all in its . . . inexplicable mystery. What was this thing? and Why was it? Of course—Turks—Turks—Turks, but then that is a mere name used to describe these creatures who were really hobgoblins and endowed with hobgoblin motives. In the olden times one could have had a certain advantage of seeing an enemy's eyes. If one was anxious about the battle one could have perhaps witnessed the anxiety of the enemy. Anything is better than a fight with an army that wears a black velvet mask of distance. . . . And now began the infantry fight at the foot of the height. . . . The whole of this sharp, hard attack was incoherent, and the strength of the drama of it was in this incoherence. . . . The Turks did not come like a flood, nor did the Greeks stand like adamant. It was simply a shifting, changing, bitter, furious struggle, where one could not place odds nor know when to run.[13]

The actual experience in Greece of love and war taught Crane more of what Henry James meant by "point of view" and what Howells meant by "complicity." In the ultimate failure of his Greek War novel, *Active Service*, his one artistic gain was, once more, a triumph in the short story, "Death and the Child." And in it are notes new to his fiction which Cora on her side and the foreign

soldiers on the other had given him. In the presence of the real
thing, the tale's hero is "edified, aghast, triumphant . . . he
remembered the pageants of carnage that had marched through the
dreams of his childhood. Love he knew; that he had confronted
alone, isolated, wondering, an individual, an atom taking the hand
of a titanic principle. Like the faintest breeze on his forehead, he
felt here the vibration from the hearts of 40,000 men." But he had
somewhere also heard something which filled in a gap in the sense
of combat in all his previous war writing: it had always lacked the
essential feel for the real presence of the missile. But now the nearby soldiers know that the bolting protagonist has not been
wounded: "Otherwise they would have heard the silken, sliding,
tender noise of the bullet, and the thud of its impact."[14]

Amid the clamor of glamor at home, however, such subtle
realities went unappreciated. As a Hearst man, Crane became more
than ever fair game. Davis had created the role of the fabulous
foreign correspondent, and Hearst blew Crane up to the same
proportions. Crane continued, of course, to register his responses to
events, and that led to a much lampooned over-emphasis on the
personal pronoun "I", especially when he crammed correspondence
into form for overseas cabling. The later, full-scale stories were far
more objective and dramatic. And, of course, Hearst exploited
Crane's name and personality all he could. Another Hearst man in
Greece, set to observe Crane observing, painted himself in a slit-
trench cautiously studying "the pale, thin face of the novelist as the
latter seated himself on an ammunition box amid a shower of shells
and casually lighted a cigarette."[15]

Of course there were howls of rage and delight from every
paragraphing Crane-baiter in America, and these were now
augmented by the enthusiastic enemies of Hearst. They rushed into
lampoon and parody. An unknown bard from Lewiston, Maine, im-
mortalized himself with a Crane war-dispatch poem:

> I have seen a battle.
> I find it very like what
> I wrote up before.
> I congratulate myself that
> I ever saw a battle.
> I am pleased with the sound of war.
> I think it is beautiful.
> I thought it would be.

> I am sure of my nose for battle.
> I did not see any war correspondents while
> I was watching the battle except
> I. [16]

But the *Denver Post* was niftiest on May 20 when its paragrapher reported: "It is said that before leaving Greece, General Miles will see everything that is to be seen at the seat of war. It will be quite an imposing spectacle when Richard Harding Davis and Stephen Crane pass before him in review."

With the country ringing with that sort of thing and New York with slander far worse, and after the encounter with Davis had made it clear what could happen to (and because of) Cora, it was obvious that there could be no return home. England seemed the obvious answer in spite of the far-distant Captain Stewart. There Crane's professional relations were cordial, his reputation enviable, and no newspaper or police war raged against him. And there, at least among Fourth Estate people, sexual taboos were loosening. Harold Frederic bigamously kept American wives in two establishments. [17] Other writers and artists, among them H. G. Wells, lived comfortably without matrimonial bonds. By early June Stephen and Cora, with a crazy retinue consisting of Mrs. Ruedy, twin Greek refugees, and a Greek puppy, had settled into "Ravensbrook Villa," Oxted, Surrey. [18] All Crane had to do was support them with his pen.

V

It had never been a commercially ready pen. Creatively, Crane was facile only when the agony of getting something "filtered" through his blood was done. He was far distant in maturity, experience, and achieved self-discovery from the reliable fecundity of masters like James and Howells who could turn out a novel a year and have time over for minor enterprises. And, of course, Greece had no more cured his crisis than Florida.

Neither could Cora help him, though she loved him dearly and doubtless did everything in her power. A fatal fact was that it was not in her power to economize. She seems to have been as improvident of outgo as Crane. The only obvious explanation for her relative business success before and after Crane's appearance in her life is that she was in a business in which money traditionally flows free and easy and spending is requisite to success.

Otherwise, their domesticity at first went beautifully—even for Crane's writing. Of course, it was convenient, perhaps mandatory, that Cora become for the neighborhood and for new friends "Mrs. Crane." Stephen went so far as to write an earlier friend, Sanford Bennett, that he had been married in Paris about August 24. Possibly he had. There was not much reason why Cora should have taken bigamy more seriously than Frederic. But it seems more likely that Miss Gilkes is right in maintaining that there was never a formal, *de jure* marriage. No marriage certificate has been found.

In this period, drawing magnificently on his slim capital of materials and psychic energy, Crane wrote a series of his finest short pieces. In spite of a month out to recuperate from a carriage accident, he produced, that year and in about the following order, "The Monster," drawing on Port Jervis; and some of his best tales: "The Bride Comes to Yellow Sky," and "Five White Mice." He banked his Greek dividend, "Death and the Child," but he failed to do much with *Active Service* despite Frederic's command. Small wonder he was exhausted at the end—and wild at his complicated failure to succeed financially with work of that quality. In the whole period he got no unborrowed money from the States: Amy Leslie had his Appleton's royalties blocked, and new things sold slowly.

Crane could not care for the holders of current English literary reputations. Swinburne bored him even worse than Henry James—who was at least resolutely kind; and George Meredith snubbed him. Crane in turn alienated both wings of the going British neo-romanticism. Like Howells, Crane had no use for the late, extravagantly lamented Stevenson. "I believe in ghosts," he said. "Mr. Stevenson has not passed away far enough. He is all around town." Neither could he care for the *fin de siècle fleurs du mal*. Except Yeats, everybody talked about Oscar Wilde "like a lot of little girls at a Sunday School party when a kid says a wicked word in a corner," said the Reverend Crane's son. "Wilde was a mildewed chump. He has a disease and they all gas about him as though there was a hell and he came up out of it," [19] said the close student of the Bowery. Instead of panic, the literary social occasion now moved him to scorn.

His English friends at this stage were, naturally enough, either other foreigners like Joseph Conrad or, as in New York, "Indians"—like Frederic, who was both. The London "Indians" were chummy and fun. But "Indian"-like, they never knew when to stop.

They blew in at random, consuming and exhausting Cora's lavish hospitality and Crane's too thin energies. The confluence of pressures made him dream again of escape—to the Klondike, to the Sudan, to someplace exotic where perhaps he might yet find himself and his way.

On February 15 the *Maine* was blown up in Havana harbor, and the U.S. government began the deadly little minuet which announced nineteenth-century wars. England, like all Europe, stirred with antagonism at the crass arrogance of the Yankees and felt assured that, if there were a war, proud Castile would slap the Yankees down. On April 11 McKinley sent the message one step short of open war to Congress, and on April 13 the House and on the sixteenth the Senate passed confirming resolutions. On the twenty-fifth McKinley declared war. Sometime before the declaration Crane had become convinced that war—the real thing this time—was certain. Desperately he begged and borrowed money and shot off to New York to join the Navy.

VI

It may have been at the naval recruitment office which rejected him that Crane learned that he was the victim of active pulmonary tuberculosis.[20] If so, neither that fact nor the rejection sent him home. He knew another way to get to the war. He went around to the *World* and took Pulitzer's shilling to go as a correspondent. After hanging around New York long enough to learn that it was an established fact that he was a dope addict, he left for Key West and the waiting, "phony" part of the war—by far the worst for a word-man. And there, amid the hordes of other correspondents, Crane discovered the impossibility of his situation. His celebrity was compounded of three contrary factors, and he was temperamentally and habitually fitted to perform publicly the role of only the falsest one. There was his literary fame—which no man ever could portray except on the pages of his art. There was his largely accidental image of glamorous correspondent, a role in the Davis mode which he necessarily refused even to approximate. And there was his notoriety as romantic satanist—a role he had elaborately played since boyhood.

Consequently he projected an image enthusiastically hated and envied by all but understanding old friends. Charles Michelson, one of them, records inimitably the wracked, sunken body, the reserved but daring psyche—who got himself dubbed "Lord Tholepin" after rumors of an English manor house drifted back:

Crane on his way to war was one of the most unprepossessing figures that ever served as a nucleus for apocryphal romances; shambling, with hair too long, usually lacking a shave, dressed like any of the deck hands, hollow-cheeked, sallow, destitute of small talk, critical if not fastidious, marked with ill-health—the very antithesis of the conquering male.[21]

In the face of the quiet soldiers and sailors Crane felt ashamed of self-important journalists. But he dug hard, too, for news where there was none, and he recorded "Jackies" saying proudly, "We've got a hot ship—a hot ship."[22] When he did finally go ashore with the Marines at Caimanera, Guantanamo Bay, however, it was the real thing—and the first American action on Cuban soil.

The steady, abrasive tension of real fear and the exhaustion of war in a tropical climate suddenly became as real as the immediate presence of people who shot real bullets at other people and deliberately killed them. With a normal tinge of modern guilt, Crane saw normally that, in one aspect, it was very like sport—and the greatest show on earth. From another point of view, there was an agony to the actual deaths more horrifying than anything he had imagined for readers.

Beer and Berryman have accepted stories that Crane "hallucinated" under the pressure and began to see things that were not there. This condition is made doubtful by the accuracy with which he registered and reported what happened. Of Marines getting ready to jump off into the brush to destroy a well from which night patrols had been harrassing them, Crane wrote, for example:

One could note the prevalance of a curious expression—something dreamy, the symbol of minds striving to tear away the screen of the future and perhaps expose the ambush of death. It is not fear in the least [but] . . . wonder. . . . Little absurd indications of time, redolent of coffee, steak, porridge, or . . . emblems of the departure of trains for Yonkers . . . now were sinister, sombre with the shadows of . . . foreseen, inexorable, invincible tragedy.

There was expert imagery, not hallucination, in the notion that Mauser bullets flew so thick about the ridge that it seemed a good player might have bagged a lot with a lacrosse stick. Nor was there hallucination in the notion that trapping guerillas in a thicket, flushing them out with shells from the supporting warship, and then shooting them down against the hillside as they broke cover in coveys was "like a grim and frightful field sport"—any more than it was hallucinatory to call the famous World War II naval victory the "Marianas Turkeyshoot." It was only that Crane at last was there,[23] really seeing combat.

Typically, the already invalid Crane went all out physically with the Marines, and he may have been in bad enough shape when other correspondents rescued him. But there was no stopping him. He picked up malaria to go with his tuberculosis and pushed along, disregarding the way quinine wracked a stomach long tender and an intestine apparently also tubercular. Eventually he was living on coffee, cigarettes, alcohol, and fruit. And still he pushed himself harder, carrying water to fighting men, tending the wounded, racing up jungly trails behind troops, exhausting himself, then staggering back miles to try to file his stories. This happened repeatedly on the days marked by the Army landing at Daiquiri on June 22, then Las Guasimas, El Caney, and San Juan Hill before the surrender of Santiago on July 14. By the end of it, Crane was even more a wreck than the Army riddled by yellow fever.

Did he try to get himself killed? Probably. One can make all kinds of guesses why, though no explanation will ever be better than a mere guess. But there seems small room for doubt about the fact of his spectacular self-neglect in the face of his multiple diseases, all of which did kill him fairly soon, though not in Cuba. Further, there are the reports of his repeatedly exposing himself to sniper fire—with the Marines and again with the Rough Riders. Davis' account of the Rough Riders incident is most revealing. Where the men were entrenching behind a ridge, Crane exposed himself in a long, white raincoat, drawing showers of bullets on the area. He ignored Col. Leonard Wood's orders to get down, wandered around smoking his pipe, and was infuriatingly careless until Davis thought of the answer:

> I knew that to Crane, anything that savored of a pose was hateful, so . . . I called, "You're not impressing anyone by doing that, Crane." As I hoped he would, he instantly dropped to his knees. When he crawled over to where we lay, I explained, "I knew that would fetch you," and he grinned, and said, "Oh, was that it?"[24]

By July 7, Crane had collapsed into delirium and was ordered evacuated by his chief. Aboard a transport the only medical attention he got was the hysterically arrogant command of a surgeon that Crane quarantine himself for yellow fever. Crewmen smuggled him stewed tomatoes. So his magnificent account, "Stephen Crane's Vivid Story of the Battle of San Juan," was datelined "In Front of Santiago, July 4, via Old Point Comfort, Va., July 13." There he watched the fascinating spectacle of genteel vacationers receiving home their country's wounded, sick, and shattered. Then he visited the *World* office and found himself fired. He had filed at least nineteen stories for the *World*, some of them the best of the war. But the office commandos were frosty. Perhaps they could not forgive him for being with the Army when Sampson smashed Cervera's fleet, or for filing Edward Marshall's story for Hearst when Ed was wounded, or for conducting campaigns against the crime of arming Americans with black powder when the Spaniards had smokeless, or for lambasting the nation's Press for giving all the glory to "Reginald Marmaduke Maurice Montmorenci Sturdevant" and ignoring the Regular Army's unknown "Michael Nolan," old professional.

Perhaps they could not forgive him for being Stephen Crane. It is imaginable that they were trying to be merciful to his tortured body. In any case, he quietly went back to Hearst. And after staying around New York long enough to collect the latest slanders (and perhaps to go to be checked by Dr. Trudeau, the famous lung man in the Adirondacks), he slipped away to see if there might not be more war in Puerto Rico. There was not, and not much real experience, though he tried "occupying" parts of the island just ahead of the American advance. Finally he slipped into Havana before it had been officially surrendered, where he was possibly liable to vengeance from the Havana police; and he knew again, for the first time since publication of *The Red Badge*, the dangerous, blessed relief of being underground.

Being so was apparently such a relief that he moved out of his hotel into an obscure boardinghouse and simply stopped communicating with anybody but the *New York Journal*, to which he sent sketches of life in Havana. Through most of September he apparently neither wrote nor picked up letters. He was reported "missing" in the papers. And missing he was—from all responsibility except to himself. Of course Cora, marooned high and dry financially as well as emotionally, became frantic. She stirred up everyone she could think of—the Crane family (with the jolt of their first news that Stephen had a "wife"); Hearst; English friends and publishers; and the United States government. Slowly, and with evident reluctance, Crane rose again to the surface.

What had been going on in Havana? Not having died, Crane may have been attempting to gather his forces to live. He may have embarked on the first self-designed regimen of his life to try to restore his squandered strength. He may have been playing for time to think things out—it seems clear that he returned to England (and even, perhaps, to Cora) with reluctance up to the final moment. Very oddly, he sailed at the end from New York to England by way of Havana. Was there another woman, as Cora intuitively feared? Or was Crane tempted to take a Rimbaudian exit from life, as Joseph Conrad's pessimism about his return suggests Conrad guessed?

One thing perhaps not taken enough into account by speculations about Crane in Havana is the symptomology of malaria. In the old American terms of "fever and ague," a malaria victim alternates agonizingly between desperate fever and bone-rattling chill. Victims recall horrid nightmares. Certainly under malarial conditions the common, discursive human mind does not function well. Thus one might explain such "complications" as those queried in the *Stephen Crane Newsletter* II (Winter 1967): 4 - 5, about an impossibly dated Crane note from "Near Santiago": "My dear sir," it said, "I have forgotten everything just now. Sorry." Precisely. Perhaps it adds a sidelight to recall that it was a soldier hospitalized in just such a condition whom the late General George Patton slapped exasperatedly in Italy. There has perhaps been too much mystification, then, about the peculiarities of Crane's behavior late in the Cuban war and in Havana. Diagnosed as having both tuberculosis and malaria, both of them debilitating and one mentally disorienting, he needed no mysterious love affair, no drugs—if indeed he could have dealt with either—to explain his behavior. Not improbably, he simply wished to die quietly.

The impressive fact about the episode is that, in the midst of his formal feeling after great pain, Crane found his imaginative vitality restored and released. He was writing steadily and with enthusiasm. He was producing short stories, poetry, and eye-witness war pieces. And his New York literary agent, Reynolds, was bombarded not only with them but with appeals to turn them quickly into lots of cash. What Crane was doing with his cash and what he intended to

do with what Reynolds was to raise simply does not appear. Cora
was not getting it, and it was only her eventual success in raising
money in England and seeing to it that Crane got it which pried
him out of Havana. Then he went to New York.

There his situation was strangely mixed. He was a kind of war
hero, having been mentioned in dispatches by the Marines for
bravery under fire as a volunteer signalman near Guantanamo. And
Davis had published his judgment that Crane was the best of the
Cuban war correspondents. Relations with publishers were easy.
The Open Boat and Other Stories had appeared just as he started
for Cuba, with an extra section of "Midnight Sketches" in the
English edition. *War Is Kind*, a second volume of verse, was
accepted, and publishers bid for the forthcoming *Active Service*.
Old friends were faithful, Howells cordial as ever; and such new
friends as James Huneker and the great painter Albert Pinkham
Ryder swam into his ken. He thought of getting a country house, or
a Texas ranch, and "duelled" with Cora across the Atlantic to get
her back.

Maybe a Poconos house or a Rio Grande ranch would have
worked—or maybe nothing would have worked. It was obvious, at
least in retrospect, that the mark of death was on Crane. Howells,
who knew it well at first hand, saw his malaria. Crane slept endlessly and dawdled listlessly when not forcing himself to simulate vigor.
And that, too, helped his enemies. Davis had to thrash a big
photographer, Thomas McCumber, for clamoring that Crane was
dying of syphilis. And the word went out among the police, where
Becker was entrenching as an underworld czar, to "get" Crane.
Friends barely saved him twice from false arrest, from blatant
"frame-ups."

Cora had prepared a *fin de siècle* nest for them in an ancient,
ruined manor house, hopefully "Indian"-proof, "Brede Place" in
England. If Becker and McCumber convinced Crane that there was
no place for him in New York, if Cora could not play the game of
hope in Texas, he could turn to the "home" he had never seen at
"Brede." If nothing better, presumably it would do to die in.

VII

There has been a great deal of controversy about "Brede." Was it
a sensible place for Crane? Obviously not: Albuquerque or
Colorado Springs or Lake Placid might have been better, or "Ed's

house" at Hartwood—or, at worst, if it had to be England, a snug flat with Cora and one servant. But that implied "taking care" of things and oneself, and neither Crane nor Cora was good at that. Left to himself, Crane thought broken-down historical "Brede" was pretty funny—but if Cora liked to be neo-romantic he was not going to disturb that any more than he did the conviction that he was all right and just needed a little motherly discipline to shape him into a machine producing saleable manuscript to pay off the bills.

Crane concealed his illness as long as he could. No torture could have induced him to explain that he was an artist or that artists have troubles not available to medicines. He shouldered the incredible tangle of debts and "arrangements" awaiting him in England and did his best to write like a machine and meet current expenses, pay off debts, and perhaps provide something for Cora's future. He turned out a lot—with surprising gems in it like *The Whilomville Stories*, and "The Upturned Face."

But creative growth was at an end. He got involved in a good deal of meaninglessness like finishing *Active Service*, trying to write a Stevensonian romance to sell and still keep his integrity by kidding it in *The O'Ruddy*, or working on *Great Battles of the World*. He put merciless pressure on himself and on his agents, especially Pinker in London, and on publishers. He finally even achieved the mere pot-boiler in a good many of those last, desperate tales on which he toiled his life away at "Brede." Not, of course, that he was unwilling. He was living out the triple vision of his own irony. He was going to die anyway, wasn't he?

Naturally there was, as witnesses have protested, plenty of fun at "Brede." Crane would have held his courage in contempt if there hadn't been. "Indians" were necessary to him, and they were invited down to "Brede" along with palefaces like Henry James, H. G. Wells, Ford Madox Hueffer, and Conrad. At Christmas there was a last, big, wonderful party at "Brede" but it ended in tragedy—and with Crane's secret out. The night before New Year's Eve he collapsed, not drunk but hemorrhaging massively from the lungs. Then he had to learn that London gossip was as vicious as New York's—there had been an "orgy" at "Brede."

He struggled to write on and let Cora put the screws on Pinker. But essentially it was the end. He kept Cora well enough deceived so that she set off on a little trip to Paris two hours before he hemorrhaged twice again on March 31. Only after that did she get seriously alarmed and start thinking of drastic measures. And of course it was too late. With infinite trouble to match his patience, she got him to Badenweiler in the Black Forest where on June 5, 1900, not yet twenty-nine, he died. Fate never let him be anything but young. In spite of everything, did it really let him be anything but rather innocent?

CHAPTER 4

"His Quality of Personal Honesty"

THE sentimentality, the artistic self-pity and gush which characterize too much of the writing about Crane since his death, would have appealed to him not at all. He meant his vision to be sharp, clear, and hard as could be, and he meant to be absolutely faithful to it. In the long run the importance of his art depends on the qualities of that vision and his great success in compelling his reader to see life as he saw. Implicit in that vision are ideas which Crane never began to make intellectually explicit. For that reason they are as difficult to discuss intelligibly as the ideas of Henry James. Few commentators have made much effort to discuss them, and perhaps only one with much success: Daniel Hoffman in *The Poetry of Stephen Crane*. Obviously, however, it is essential to every understanding of an artist and his art that such informing commitments be explained as well as can be.

But once again an examiner runs into a fog of ignorance about Crane's life, in this case the life of his mind. What did Crane ever read? More important, what did he read before he wrote the major works? The darkness is lightened almost solely by Beer's records of hearsay recollected after twenty-five years or so and by scholarly conjecture. Even when Crane has mentioned (or is said to have mentioned) a book, it is generally hard to know whether he read it. Tolstoi was his favorite author, he testified: was that because he was Howells's favorite? *War and Peace* went on and on like Texas, he is supposed to have remarked: had he read it through? Zola's *Nana* is "honest" and "Zola is a sincere writer but—is he much good?" Beer quotes Crane long after he wrote *Maggie:* had he read *Nana* even then—or heard that he should and glanced at it? The late Professor Lars Åhnebrink, in his careful study of Crane in *The Beginnings of Naturalism in American Literature*, shows by sensitively chosen parallels that Crane might have learned much from a number of Continental authors. But that sort of inference

75

from British readers made Crane explode—though their remarks at
literary teas were probably much more *avant garde*-ishly com-
plimentary in intent than he realized. Such questions drove him
toward anti-intellectual postures: had he read Mallarmé? Well, no,
he didn't know much about "Irish" authors.

The one thing about which I think we can be morally, though not
evidentially, certain is that Crane read avidly in the great contemporary household literary magazines—for which we possess no intellectual parallel in the middle-brow culture of our time—at least
from Claverack days (1888) forward. Everybody else in his social
and intellectual class read *Harper's Monthly* and *Harper's Weekly*,
the *Century, Scribner's,* the *Atlantic,* and perhaps the *North
American Review.* They typically took ideas and the intellectual
news seriously in those journals. Crane would work for McClure
and must have read his smart new magazine after 1893. Indeed, by
that date if not earlier he must have been reading everything he
could get his hands on, studying it for potential markets. As a
youngster he published not only in newspapers but in magazines
like *Truth, Arena,* the *Plumbers' Trade Journal,* the *Bookman,* the
Philistine, Cosmopolitan, and *Town Topics,* among others.

Since "magazining"—not book publication—was the principal
source of literary income in his time, it is a virtual cinch that Crane
read everybody, and a lot of nobodies, domestic and foreign, in the
magazines. He could not have helped learning how they worked,
both masters and hacks. Panning that gold might yield solid returns
to the Crane scholar. The reason why, of course, is that there *had* to
be the place where Crane got the education he all too obviously got
nowhere else.

I

Perhaps one way out of the fog is to rise above it and try to see
Crane in the aerial perspective of relationships to the movements in
thought and attitude of his time, to see him in configuration with
the history of ideas. The most prominent feature on the intellectual
landscape of the age was disillusion. Then occurred that crisis of
idealism, the failure to recover from which marks the end of an era
as well as a century and the beginning of "modernity." From the
peaks of Jacksonian, transcendentalist, evangelical, humanitarian,
romantic, and Utopian optimism following the era of good-feeling,
Americans had been dropped with a jolt to the disconcerting

realities of the Mexican War, the European disasters of 1848, and the moral squalor of the Compromise of 1850. Then came fifteen years of political failure and tragic civil war. Then disastrous cultural revolution in the industrialization and urbanization of culture while the West was raped and the very population altered by the mysteries of massive immigration. In the midst of all this came the shattering ideas as much symbolically as necessarily associated with the names of Darwin and Marx.

The result is the oft-told story of the "Victorian Dilemma." It is a tale of deflation, the reduction of idealism. " 'Twas disillusion upon disillusion," said Robert Frost in "The White-Tailed Hornet." "We were lost piecemeal to the animals, / Like people thrown out to delay the wolves." And among intellectual Americans this process hit its nadir in Crane's time (and largely among those who were his contemporaries like Frederic, Norris, Dreiser, Gertrude Stein, Edwin Arlington Robinson, Masters, and Frost). Most of the others lived to come to some sort of terms with that process which would strike perhaps its deepest notes in *The Mysterious Stranger Manuscripts* and *The Education of Henry Adams*. Crane could not.

It is relevant to Crane's personal case to notice that, in a way, the crisis had been caused by a failure in spiritual resources. Since the Renaissance a steadily increasing intellectual community had been living off the spiritual capital of Christendom. Many efforts to revive, reform, or find a vital substitute for it had failed, and so, finally, had the heritage. In his own way Crane was to recapitulate that process.

Immediately, of course, the crisis for most Americans was religious. The vital crisis sprang from the threat of Darwinism to reduce man to complete, mere animality and find the key to his condition in a Machiavellian ethic of pure power. God seemed excluded from the universe; so did spirituality and meaning from the life of man. The ultimate reduction of all thought to a pure, hard naturalism impended. No metaphysics would there approach reality. Cosmology, teleology, and anthropology would fall to the aimless collisions of chance with matter until the triumph of entropy in designless stasis.

No American writer ever wholly accepted that ultimate, though Robinson Jeffers the poet of "inhumanism" perhaps comes closest. Confronted by that prospect, virtually every thinker has wished to reconstitute idealism as well as he could or dared, from the minima of E. A. Robinson's "Credo," Dreiser's triumphant confusion, or

Woodbridge's "natural teleology" up through infinite varieties of compromise to various forms of complete neo-ideality. Historically, in the decades prior to Crane there had tended to be a response according to generations. One tended to fly to quick hopes, if, like Whitman, Melville, or Lowell, he'd come to maturity amid the ancient comforts.

If, however, one had spent his youth secure but found his young maturity threatened by the new thought, the case was interestingly altered. He tended to postpone decision, to take time to let things settle, and make only minimal decisions meanwhile. He became, perhaps for decades, perhaps for life, an agnostic. That was generally true for the generation more or less thirty in 1870—Twain, Howells, and the James brothers, Peirce, Wright, young Holmes, and the Adams brothers. But what of Crane's group, a generation born into the newness and presented with compromise against which to revolt? The evidence is clear that it was sorely tempted to pay the price, no matter what, and go the whole way. Some eventually announced, impermanently or imperfectly, that they had gone and become total naturalists. In the works of all, the struggle toward or against it is recorded. And, though that does not categorically make him a "naturalist," it is true of Stephen Crane also.

All these tendencies, with special variations for every individual, were operative in the worlds of family, churches, schools, colleges, books and journalism—in the whole climate of thought and feeling in which Crane grew up. Heuristically it may be helpful to see the ideas and literary attitudes of the time in an interlocking figure of these themes short of naturalism.

The simplest way to take the new thought was to be antiintellectual—to reject it entirely. Religiously this led to the Fundamentalism which William Jennings Bryan espoused at the Scopes trial. That rejection characteristically went hand in hand with an emotional refusal to see that rural mores did not fit urban-industrial circumstances. And, in spite of itself, Fundamentalism was keyed to the low-brow features of popular culture—in literature especially to those ancient clichés of romantic sentimentality and heroicism which Howells mocked in his famous simile of the grasshopper. That was the sort of religion and, one suspects, the sort of culture Crane inherited through his mother from the Pecks.

Far more respectable intellectually was the neo-idealism of a Whitman or the "Personalist" philosophers of Syracuse University; or of Sidney Lanier, or Lowell; of Minot J. Savage or John Fiske; of

William Graham Sumner or Lester Ward. It might go all the way to Transcendentalism or beyond with Whitman, to a neo-idealistic Christianity with Lanier, Savage, or Fiske. It might erect a mystique of individualism with the "hard" Social Darwinism of Sumner or a mystique of group solidarity with Ward. Howells as Tolstoian was strongly tempted Ward's way. And neo-idealism keyed reality to neo-romanticism in the arts because they were characteristically parallel reactionary modes of thought and feeling. Neo-romanticism was admittedly not a true continuation of Wordsworth and Coleridge, Scott, Shelley, and Keats. Forced to the wall, its adherents confessed that they no longer believed as the Romantics had. They just wanted arts, particularly a literature, into which they could escape from the real world. They wished to forget care, doubt, worry, confusion, and pain and live imaginatively in free sentiment, the exotic, sublime, chivalric, magical, and strenuous. Rider Haggard and then Stevenson and Du Maurier were their men—and the George Eliot of *Romola* their woman. They characteristically held political, social, economic views to match.

The agnostics, on the other hand, suffered the curious advantages of their lack of comfort, their need for courage. Deprived of abstraction and generalization, they had to descend to the concrete particular. Deprived of the divine and spiritual, they descended to the human (and bore resolutely there, refusing to be depressed to the animal). Deprived of the ideal, the sublime, the heroic, they had left the average, the commonplace, the ordinary—for better or worse, they were wed to the common. It was this allegiance which made realism attractive, natural, perhaps almost inevitable for them. It also made their sympathies characteristically democratic, humane, and contemporaneous—and so revisionist, or reformist, perhaps in some way socialistic. In pattern, ignoring all variation and aberrations such as those of Henry and Brooks Adams, one can say that *realist* implied democrat, humanitarian, sceptic, reformer, and anti-imperialist. *Neo-romantic* implied aristocrat, racist, "hard" Darwinist, conservative, and imperialist. And amid all these congeries within American life, immensely more fluid than any scheme could show, Stephen Crane was fated to be a Seeker after the secret of his own vision.

II

Nobody was wholly, purely any of those "types." Everybody was a mixture—and himself. What was Stephen Crane? Again, for lack

of evidence there is much one shall never know. And, because of
Crane's perpetual youth, there has to be less to know than in a case
of achieved maturity. Yet there are interesting and helpful leads
toward understanding the intellectual qualities of that vision which
was central to Crane and his art.

The first and most essential themes of his thought are religious.
For life-reasons, his religion was necessarily rebellious. That did
not, however, prevent it from being serious. On the contrary, he absolutely refused to have the blasphemy bowdlerized from *The Black
Riders* even though it was to be his first regularly published book;
the publisher could keep it in or return the manuscript. As Hoffman
intelligently and originally shows, it was the frontier, Calvinistic,
minatory evangelicism of the Pecks against which Stephen revolted
violently. The behaviorism of his father's moral tracts and his
father's commitment to the church as institution Stephen also rejected—but not his father's gentle intuition of God's love per-
vading, hidden behind His objective universe, supporting all, quick
and tender in mercy.

Proceeding with the inevitable pain of confusion added to the
wrath of revolt, Crane groped his way toward a religion of his own.
The point which has eluded perhaps most commentators is that he
was most *revolté*, most exasperating, most agonized—and probably
most creative—when he insisted on taking the heart of the family
code seriously. If, instead of practicing bourgeois, institutional
respectability, one practiced the virtues of St. Francis and Sir Philip
Sidney in Port Jervis or Asbury Park, what then? If one didn't practice those directly, why pretend? Why are non-respectable sins
which unite one with common humanity not better than respectable·
sins which degrade and divide the brotherhood of man? That, one
must think, is pretty surely the logic of Stephen Crane in tutelage to
mother, family, schools.

He never adolescently denied the reality of sin—his sin. He took
obvious pride in confessing himself a bad boy, the family black
sheep. His chosen position, however, committed him to one of the
permanent themes of his thought. It was that, fully recognizing the
slippery multivalences of truth, one must be as absolutely honest as
he could. An early reviewer put his finger on an essentially Cranean
quality when he spoke of *Maggie*'s "daring and terrible directness
which in its iconoclasm is the very characteristic of rugged undisciplined strength in a youth of genius.[1]" Crane meant to smash
icons. But there was that blend Harvey Wickham noted in him of

"self-depreciation coupled with arrogance" and stimulated by "fear of ridicule, especially of his own."[2]

Emerson spoke to Crane as to so many of his targets—"the young men of America." From the wall of the old Art Students' League Building which his poverty inhabited, for instance, Crane copied off the Emersonian motto: "Congratulate yourself if you have done something strange and extravagant and broken the monotony of a decorous age."[3] But there was always his need for a saving balance. And so he defined himself in famous words to John Northern Hilliard:

> . . . I understand that a man is born into the world with his own pair of eyes, and he is not at all responsible for his vision—he is merely responsible for his quality of personal honesty. To keep close to this honesty is my supreme ambition. There is sublime egotism in talking of honesty. I, however, do not say that I am honest. I merely say that I am as nearly honest as a weak mental machinery will allow. This aim in life struck me as being the only thing worth while. A man is sure to fail at it, but there is something in the failure.[4]

That arrogance of a self-depreciating iconoclasm also informed Crane's treatment of the tradition from his father which he readapted for his most enduring and fundamental ideal: the Christian gentleman. Since there had been Americans, sensitive men had worked to reconcile that major ideal to American conditions.[5] There are plenty of data to show that Stephen Crane joined their ranks after his fashion. The plainest evidence appears in his confessional letters to Miss Nellie Crouse of Akron, Ohio, written just as *The Red Badge of Courage* made him an international celebrity.

In capsule, when the Aristotelian pattern of the hero was syncretized with the Christian picture of the saint, the resulting chivalric ideal became a beautiful vision reserved for the nobility. In Renaissance times Castiglione's notions of the intellectual and esthetic cultivation of the courtier met in England with the rising power of the landed gentry and with the Protestant theory of individual responsibility to convert chivalry into the ideal of the English gentleman. A series of fine compromises secured the values which made England great. Not blood alone (for the class was relatively fluid) but virtue, not wealth alone but cultivation, not manners alone but service to others characterized the complete gentleman. Love and, above all, service to Cross and Crown, to land and house, to tenant as to family: distinguished, objective, unselfish service was the *beau idéal* of the English Gent.—For the American colonial period, the idea was permanently set by Sir Richard Steele, whose *The Christian Hero* (1701) became the ideal opposed to Chesterfield by a myriad American magazinists, by Tyler's *The Contrast* for the early Republic, by Fenimore Cooper for the Romantic age. The magazines Crane read were replete with studies of the theme. It appears even in Conrad.

Amid the fluidities and erosions of colonial American life, that ideal was of utmost social importance. To save its essence for the waxing democracy of post-Revolutionary America had been of central intellectual concern to minds as diverse as those of Jefferson and Emerson. Demonstrably the ideal had lived among descendants of Jasper and Stephen Crane quite conscious of debts to family and tradition. By 1896 the then current Stephen was trying to prove to a chic and pretty girl that he was not in the popular sense a Bohemian and that a true view of things exposed the foolish exhaustion of both the Bohemian and the conventional views.

In no very logical sequence, Crane let Miss Nellie Crouse see the pattern of his ideal. Emptiness and mere conceit make up too nearly all the core of what Society values. Therefore, he dislikes the "society man" and especially the "society matron," with the peculiar ironlike quality of their thick-headedness and the wild exuberance of their vanity. Together they create "the social crisis" (apparently the demand to flaunt one's vanity) which makes Crane "gibber" and fail humiliatingly. The society man is too often an "awful chump" or a "duffer" because his courage, courtesy, and integrity are all for show: "There is an enormous majority who, upon being insured of safety from detection—become at once the most unconventional of peoples." As for "the hordes who hang upon the outskirts of good society and chant 143 masses per day to the social gods and think that because they have money they are well-bred—for such people I have a scorn which is very deep and very intense."

Crane's instinct for his subject was traditional and precise. "Form really is truth, simplicity," he told Miss Crouse about manners. Again, "I swear by the real aristocrat. The man whose forefathers were men of courage, sympathy, and wisdom, is usually one who will stand the strain whatever it may be. He is like a thoroughbred horse. His manes may be high and he will do a lot of jumping often but in the crisis he settles down and becomes the most reliable and enduring of created things." And that he thought such fortitude would ever be called upon he repeatedly made clear in this odd epistolary courtship.

Mankind he thought doomed to vanity "and the inherent indolence and cowardice which is the lot of all. . . ." Not even "high aims and things" could save. Most idealists "strike me as about the worst and most penetrating kind of bore I know." They really mean vanity, ". . . and there is a ridiculous quality to me in all high ambitions, of men who mean to try to make themselves great because they think it would [be] so nice to be great, to be admired, to be stared at by the mob." Finally, even the very few who are sincere are doomed:

Tolstoy's aim is, I suppose—I believe—to make himself good. It is an incomparably quixotic task for any man to undertake. He will not succeed; but he will even succeed more than he can ever himself know, and so at his nearest point to success he will be proportionately blind. This is the pay of this kind of greatness.

Was this mere blackness, defeatism? Crane had already tried to assure Nellie Crouse that it was not. He admitted to being "minded to die in my thirty-fifth year." That was all he could stand. "I don't like to make wise remarks on the aspect of life but I will say that it doesn't strike me as particularly worth the trouble. The final wall of the wise man's thought however is Human Kindness of course. If the road of disappointment, grief, pessimism, is followed far enough, it will arrive there. Pessimism itself is only a little, little way, and moreover it is ridiculously cheap. The cynical mind is an uneducated thing." To be "as kind and as just as may be" is "the solitary pleasure of life." For what life offered finally was not pleasure but "a sincere, desperate, lonely battle" against ". . . the majestic forces which are arrayed against man's true success—not the world—the world is silly changeable, any of its decisions can be reversed—but man's own colossal impulses more strong than chains. . . ."

It was of a piece with the tragedy of Crane's life and vision that he failed to enlist Miss Crouse to fight beside him. The vision, and perhaps Crane's reputation, frightened her in spite of his assurance that he found the society *girl* "charming."[6] It was a frightening vista, taken from a point of vantage only available to the irony which follows upon bitter disillusion. Little wonder Crane found no girl ready to share it; to understand it without help required a Reinhold Niebuhr.

The wonder is that there has been so little remark on the intrinsically aristocratic *and* Christian qualities of Crane's vision. One can understand a Crane in a post-Kirkegaardian world more readily than before. Only a man who had seen through to the conceit and hypocrisy behind "the world" and then turned his disillusion ironically upon his own conceit as the critic of other men's sin could have reached Crane's viewpoint. Taken seriously, as an earnest, gifted, and isolated preacher's orphan might take them, the ideals of the Christian gentleman easily exposed the follies of the world. All the rest might come from the mere turning of his honesty back upon himself.

Despite Hoffman's pioneering and some very interesting articles[7] (excluding some fashionable but non-serious efforts at mythical interpretation), Crane's relations with Christianity remain to be definitively studied. The preacher's kid of course commanded a full stock of biblical and churchly allusion, rhythm, and imagery. At the same time, the rebel was most likely of all to be aware when and why he employed them. He could revolt, that is, but not escape. He had nothing but contempt for the charity-working "Christianity as seen around town."[8] But that was because it was "seen"—and because he thought it not Christian. To his own compassion there was no conscious limit: "One of Stephen Crane's characteristics was a haunting solicitude for the comfort and welfare of other people," recalled Frank Noxon, "especially those of narrow opportunity. He thought about it as one thinks about an art or craft, developing a style and inventing original methods."[9] Obviously this compassion was a controlling feature of his literary imagination as well.

That solicitude and perhaps, as Van Wyck Brooks suggests,[10] some deep psychological need of his generation to know squalor and chaos, sent Crane to study the Bowery. But other impulses came also from his relation to gentility. That *méfiance* which prompted Crane to talk Bowery dialect to a sweet young socialite and to treat a midnight streetwalker like a duchess for the benefit of an unwanted literary admirer, also a minister's son,[11] had deep roots. Partly it was disgust at social hypocrisy. But partly also it was Crane's response to feeling *déclassé*. To repeat, as a type the American *déclassé* author has never been studied. Yet his ranks are full and fascinating. They include, among others, Freneau, Cooper,

Poe, Emerson, Hawthorne, Melville, Twain, Frank Norris, and Scott Fitzgerald beside Crane. How much of Ishmael's "hypo" did Crane take down to the Bowery? And was Crane the first American in whom the *déclassé* became also the *déraciné*?

III

Those and perhaps less scrutable temperamental or psychic factors lay behind his sense that the essence of life is war. No one has apparently ever challenged the observation that this was Crane's basic sense of life. The evidence is overwhelming. And, if there be no clear explanation of the origin of his idea, he succeeds so well in finding war in every relation of man to man, to woman, to nature, and to institutions that he leaves his reader convinced. The only way to avoid Crane's conviction is to step out of his world into one more tender-minded. War, says Vernall, Crane's *alter ego* in "War Memories": ". . . it is simply life . . ." *Maggie* begins with a skirmish—the slum kids are playing "King of the Hill" with vicious fervor. From first to last in Crane's serious expression, esthetic or not, the vision of war is at the center. One could document it almost endlessly and at random. It lies at the heart of every significant fiction. It is the *donnée* of Crane's imagination.

If one simply accepts that "given" and adds the obvious features of his boyhood, it is easy to see how young Stephen became fascinated by the phenomena of fear and courage. The frail kid who would catch barehanded any ball anybody could pitch in Asbury Park; who pegged down to second base no matter if the pain doubled him up at Syracuse; and who coached, and played quarterback for a flying-wedge, help-the-runner town football team, needed no "actual" war to teach him fear and courage. He would find his knowledge confirmed at the wars.

Crane knew about the physical phenomena of fear in many guises—the panic of *The Red Badge*, the "eels of despair [which] lay wet and cold against [the] back" of the New York Kid in "The Five White Mice"[12]—but he was mainly inclined to define and dramatize fear as anything the coward permitted to interfere with courage. And he achieved an exact and useful definition of courage which anticipates that of Ernest Hemingway.

This definition properly occurs most overtly in non-fictional pieces. He loved locomotive engineers, for instance. A Greek who, wounded, persisted in driving one through artillery barrages Crane called "a daisy." But, reporting for McClure on "The Scotch Express," he said it just right:

It should be a well-known fact that, all over the world, the engine-driver is the finest type of man that is grown. He is the pick of the earth. He is altogether more worthy than the soldier, and better than the men who move on the sea in ships. He is not paid too much; nor do his glories weight his brow; but for outright performance, carried on constantly, coolly, and without elation, by a temperate, honest, clear-minded man, he is the further point. And so the lone human at his station in a cab, guarding money, lives, and the honor of the road, is a beautiful sight. The whole thing is aesthetic. [13]

To put it that way, finding the highest and best—and the beautiful—in the daily commonplace was the essence of literary realism. But Crane did not always put it so. His revised account of the action in which he himself achieved heroism—the Marine raid at Guantanamo—is worth quoting from at length. It contains other notes:

Then the bullets began to snap, snap, snap, at his head, while all the woods began to crackle like burning straw. I could lie near and watch the face of the signalman, illumed as it was by the yellow shine of lantern-light, and the absence of excitement, fright, or any emotion at all on his countenance was something to astonish all theories out of one's mind. The face was in every instance merely that of a man intent upon his business, the business of wig-wagging into the gulf of night where a light on the *Marblehead* was seen to move slowly.

These times on the hill resembled, in some ways, those terrible scenes on the stage—scenes of intense gloom, blinding lightning, with a cloaked devil or assassin or other appropriate character muttering deeply amid the awful roll of the thunderdrums. It was theatric beyond words: one felt like a leaf in this booming chaos, this prolonged tragedy of the night. Amid it all one could see from time to time the yellow light on the face of a preoccupied signalman. . . .

Clancy had to return to the top of the ridge and outline himself and his flag against the sky . . . as soon as the Spaniards caught sight of this silhouette, they let go like mad at it. To make things more comfortable for Clancy, the situation demanded that he face the sea and turn his back to the Spanish bullets. This was a hard game, mark you—to stand with the small of your back to volley firing. Clancy thought so. Everybody thought so. We all cleared out of his neighborhood. . . .

I watched his face, and it was as grave and serene as that of a man writing in his own library. He was the very embodiment of tranquility in occupation. He stood there amid the animal-like babble of the Cubans, the crack of rifles, and the whistling snarl of the bullets, and wigwagged . . . without heeding anything but his business. There was not a single trace of nervousness or haste.

To say the least, a fight at close range is absorbing as a spectacle. No man wants to take his eyes from it until that time comes when he makes up his mind to run away. To deliberately stand up and turn your back to a battle is in itself hard work. To deliberately stand up and turn your back to a battle and hear immediate evidences of the boundless enthusiasm with which a large company of the enemy shoot at you from an adjacent thicket is, to my mind at least, a very great feat. [14]

There are true ambivalences of treatment and appeal in this account between dry, rather deprecating, and lush, heroic tones. They evidence a real ambivalence in the author. He was torn between loyalties both natural and preferential to the emotions and modes of the realists and those of the Rooseveltian, "strenuous life" neo-romanticists.

IV

On or about December 1, 1895, W. D. Howells received one of the most extraordinary fan letters in a long literary life not devoid of surprise. He had favorably reviewed in his *Harper's Weekly* column a book called *Red Men and White* written by a younger friend to whom he had given literary advice nearly ten years before. The letter read:

I have just got through with reading your "Life and Letters" on Wister—For one who protests so much ignorance you come more nearly telling just what Wister is doing *("TRUTH"—)* than any other fellow who is set in judgment on things of the sort. Wister is a great man and it gives me comfort to know that he will help me by his success to make people see *"the thing"* which is my soul. When one thinks that when I drew 'scouts—soldiers—injuns'—it was the worst of form to treat such 'red eyed' red covered—unreal stuff—it gives me courage to have you think Wister will finally bring home to such as you—*the thing*—the truth—however much you may not care for it. I wish that this had happened before Thanksgiving.

Frederic Remington [15]

With full allowance for temperament, Remington's anger half veiled in praise reflected resentments held by a group of Americans

to whom Howells had indeed given scant consideration. They em-
bodied the spirit of a gambling culture. They were lovers of action
and competition—of pitting oneself against nature, against pain
and pressure, against other men. They were sportsmen. As climbers,
hunters, and fishermen they loved wildness. As boxers and
wrestlers, rowers and runners, inventive developers of baseball,
football, basketball, and hockey, they were changing the face and
tone of American life, most especially in the colleges. Their popular
following grew phenomenally. Sports expressed the essence of
American culture perhaps more directly than anything else. And
they were beginning to achieve a literature published representatively in the magazines of the House of Harpers from which
Howells was parting just as Stephen Crane came seriously on the
scene. Henry Mills Alden, in defiance both of his friend Howells
and of his own literary convictions, was printing the fiction of
Wister, the nonfiction of Roosevelt, and the pictures of Remington.

That was not a literature, as it was not a quality of life, attractive
to the Dean of American Letters. He was prepared to agree that
sports were healthful and emotionally appropriate for the young.
But he hoped they would grow up and sober down. He hoped
Americans would grow away from frontier bully-boy muscularity
toward civilization, would leave gambling for creativity, passion for
discipline, competition for cooperation. To him the most shocking
fact about American life was precisely that it *was* a shrieking World
of Chance, brutalized, corrupted, and too often blood-spattered by
dog-eat-dog ethics. His long war with the neo-romantics was being
fought on one side over just that issue. His delight in "banging the
Babes of Romance about" rose from his derision of the ridiculous
sentimentalities, the flossy pomposities and foolish sublimities of
century-old clichés. But ethically he was determined to raise his
public to the highest level of sensitive and responsible civilization.
At best the sportsmen and their writers looked atavistic to Howells.
At worst they looked as Theodore Roosevelt hunting bears for sport
looked to the memorialist of *Mark Twain in Eruption.*

How things looked to Howells, of course, made a great difference
to Stephen Crane. Crane felt "indelibly indebted" not only for
friendship but for literary guidance and enlightenment. He had rejoiced to enlist in "the beautiful war" for realism, and he gave
thanks that experience proved him allied neither "to the Chump in
Art or even to the Semi-Chump in Art." [16] The fact that Crane dared
use such sporty language with the Dean evidenced two important

aspects of their relationship, however. Both understood that Crane was to be no little Howells, but wholly Stephen Crane. And among his many intellectual tensions was that between the pole of Howells's complex, mature vision of a responsible and humane life and art and the pole of the Remington-Wister-TR doctrine.

The most contagious form of neo-romanticism, the Rooseveltian attitude was the one least vulnerable to the ironies of Howells, Twain, and Veblen. It probably played a decisive role in the defeat of the realists in their fight for American taste in the 1890s. More significantly, its mood was to sweep the nation into the Spanish-American and Philippine wars, into imperialism, international adventure, and eventual major power status. A muscular, buoyant, college-bred elite, represented primarily but by no means uniquely in .TR, had sprung from the Gilded Age. After many terms in the presidency since Jackson, observed Howells upon Roosevelt's ascension to the White House, the "simple men" had been fated by conditions in the republic to give way again to the "gentle men" [he carefully separated the words]. In the '90s that elite was wooing the psyche of the nation preparatory to taking over power. The inherent conflict between realism and all it implied and muscular neo-romanticism was what Remington, Yale football player, bankrupt stockman, and avowed "romantic"[17] was finally getting at.

The attractions of "the strenuous life" for Crane were many, but compromised. His sense of war and cult of courage had much to do with it. The perplexities of Silas Lapham or Basil March might be real enough, even agonizing, in the moral context of civilization. But other impulses, admittedly uncivilized, stirred Crane's imagination. Striving to make copy of nothing much on the way to Greece, he wrote an odd, revealing bit into an account of the movements of a British battleship's boat:

> Down in the launch . . . there was a middy who was a joy. He was smaller than a sparrow, but—my soul—how bright and Napoleonic and forcible he was! . . . She would be a fool of a Mother who would trust him in a pantry where there were tarts, and his big sister can box his ears for some years to come, but of course there is no more fiery-hearted scoundrel in the fleet of the Powers than this babe. Of course he would drop to his knees and pray his Admiral a hundred prayers if by this he could be at his station on the *Camperdown,* and have her move into action immediately. Against what? Against anything. This is of the traditions that perforce are in the breast of the child. . . . If another child of the *Camperdown* should steal this child's knife he might go to a corner and perhaps almost shed tears, but

no hoary admiral can dream of the wild slaughter and Hades on the bosom
of the sea that agitate this babe's breast. He is a damned villain. And yet
may the God of Battle that sits above the smoke watch over this damned
villain and all bright, bold, little damned villains like him![18]

Something of the same neo-romantic *panache* occasionally overcame Crane in Cuba—or when, especially at the end of his life, he
wrote in desperate haste for money. Experience, however, always
restored the balance his irony demanded. The awful bathos which
overcame the braggart, soon-defeated Greeks set Crane to writing
amazingly like the Hemingway who was to become in important
ways so amazingly like him anyway. He interviewed defeated Greek
soldiers, and one much impressed him:

In the photograph galleries in Athens there are many portraits of bearded
gentlemen in kilts festooned with 500 yards of cartridge belt and gripping
their Gras rifles ferociously. . . . I know that type too, and I have never
seen them do anything. Generally speaking, they are a pack of humpty-
dumptys. But this brown-faced, quiet lad, with his lamb-like eyes and gently considerate ways, I know him too, and he will stick to a trench, and stick
and stick and go without water and food and fight long and still stick until
the usual orders come to fall back. . . .

The soldier answers his question:

"I am a soldier. I have been fortunate enough to have been wounded for
Greece. I have lived on nothing practically for months, and marched many
miles and fought a few battles. I have a right to name any man whom I am
sure has not done his duty by Greece, and I name the crown prince."
  "Did he not say, or at least was he not reported to have said at Domokos
that there he would stand or fall with his men?"
  "Yes, such was the report. But where is Domokos now? In the hands of
the Turks. . . . These quotable sentiments are sometimes unfortunate. I
know from experience."
  "Why?"
  "Well, when I left Athens there was a considerable celebration by my
family and friends. Tears and flowers, added to a Spartan injunction from
my mother. I believe I replied with a Spartan sentence too. It is very
difficult."[19]

If irony cut down Crane's romanticism, so did compassion. His
"haunting solicitude" for others shattered any capacity for
smugness he might have had. It reached out to the physical suffer-

ing of animals and people. War-wounded and refugees naturally moved him deeply. Of the Greeks he wrote, "Their plight makes a man hate himself for being well fed and having some place to go. . . . There is no food. . . . It is a case for the opening of skies, but no skies open. I wish I knew what is to become of these poor people."[20] He found it useful to advise his readers that, "There is more of this sort of thing in war than glory and heroic death, flags, banners, shouting, and victory."[21] And, of course, the same thing went for psychic pain. He described the heartbreak of Cuban wives and children when Spanish fathers were forcibly repatriated at the end of the war. It was easy to say: " 'Serves them right; why didn't they take up with men of their own people, instead of with Spaniards?' But, after all—and after all—and again after all, it is human agony and human agony is not pleasure."[22]

V

On the other hand, Crane's vision and temperament were too aristocratic (and perhaps too natively Calvinist) to let him sympathize with the democratic or Tolstoian humanitarianism of a Garland, Howells, or Edward Bellamy. The bitter humor of his suggestion that an American Academy consist wholly of Edwin Markham has been lamentably misread.[23] One of Crane's last journalistic efforts, this was a bit of "paragraphing" sarcastically expressing his contempt of the very idea of American "immortals," in spite of the fact "that we can show more fine old litterateurs with manes of snow-white hair than any country on the face of the globe" and have a noble race of college presidents busily raiding the wealth of Chicago. But he was equally contemptuous of the Whitmanian:

And what then? One's thoughts instinctively turn to Edwin Markham. Mr. Markham is of that virile manhood which expresses itself by appearing in public in its shirt sleeves; a strong man, Mark ye; no apish child of fashion; a veritable eagle of freedom, and, withall, kindly, tender to the little lame lamb—I, bold, yet gentle, defiant of all convention, and yet simple in his manner even to kings. Such a man is Edwin Markham.

Very good. We have made a fair start. We have one leonine old man in his shirt sleeves. We proceed, much encouraged. Who is worthy to take a place by the side of the illustrious coatlessness? Let us make haste. The name of W. D. Howells occurs to somebody. But, no; he wears collars. It is known; it is common talk. He has never had his photograph taken while enwrapped in a carelessly negligent bath towel. In the name of God, let us have virility; let us look for the wild, free son of nature. Mark Twain? At first it seems that he would have a chance. He growls out his words from the very pit of his stomach and is often uncivil to strangers. But, no; he, too, wears collars and a coat.

For a moment we are stunned with a sense of defeat. But, no; an inspiration comes. Why have forty members to an American Academy? Let us have only one. Call Markham; frame him up; give him a constitution and a set of by-laws; let him convene himself and discuss literary matters. Then we have an American Academy.[24]

This was the Crane who observed of another sentimental reformer that Miss Frances Willard's "affair with Miss Willard should be stopped by the police."[25]

Always alienated from the folksy, Gospel of Wealth-worshiping *bourgeoisie*, Crane was typically marooned between the aristocratic neo-romantics and their realist-reformer opponents. The one seemed brutally fatuous, the other sentimental. Mrs. Howells was quite right, he told one inquiring lady, that he had "no opinion of missions." He disliked the whole relationship. Briefly in the bush with Cuban partisans, he had witnessed their incredible capacity to endure hunger, fatigue, and pain. With the army, he saw their equal uselessness as regular soldiers. The Cuban fighting man, he concluded, "exists with the impenetrable indifference or ignorance of the greater part of the people in an ordinary slum. Everybody knows that the kind of sympathetic charity which loves to be thanked is often grievously disappointed and wounded in tenement districts. . . . The Cubans accept our stores in something of this way."[26] And, he implies, that is as it should be in both cases; it is in the nature of things.

Inevitability did not, however, lend glamor to the deprived in Crane's eyes. He could sympathize with the pathos of their condition. Investigating "Opium's Varied Dreams"[27] for his study of New York, he found that it was "the 'sporting' class" of the Tenderloin which most took it up—"cheap actors, race track touts, gamblers, and the different kinds of confidence men. . . ." He found them neither glamorous nor victimized. They saw no gorgeous dreams, he held. But they found "a fine languor, a complete mental rest. . . . Wrong departs, injustice vanishes; there is nothing but a quiet harmony of all things—until the next morning." Of course this "lie" is most eagerly embraced by "the people of the Tenderloin: they who are at once supersensitive and hopeless . . .

but they awake to find the formidable labors of life grown more formidable"—and hit the pipe again. In short, "the root of Bowery life," as he told Mrs. Howells's enquiring friend, was "a sort of cowardice."[28] That was what his long investigation of the poor had taught him.

By the same token, he was not in the least impressed with the innate nobility of the common man. The heroism of individual Greek soldiers had utterly shamed their poltroon of a Crown Prince, Crane thought. But he was most negatively affected by the sight of a civilian demagogue's failure to manipulate a disgruntled crowd to turn the disaster to political account. There are buried memories of the post-Periclean contemptibility of the *demos* in Crane's story of how "the man in the white hat" brought his mob to the palace and left it agitating before a single evzone sentry while he went inside. There rose "the audible machinery, the temper of the people, revolving and revolving toward turbulence":

> Once the humming of voices in its crescendo almost reached the point of action. Then this kilted soldier, this simple child of the hills, darted a look at the crowd, and this look was so full of scorn, deep and moving scorn, that it must have been felt to the pits of their stomachs. He stooped and picked from the ground a handful of pebbles. He raised his arm and, still profoundly deliberate and with supreme disdain, this solitary figure on the palace steps flung the handful of pebbles straight into the upturned faces of the Athenians.[29]

Likewise the racism and its correlative imperialism of his age affected Crane ambiguously. From Cuba he wrote that Americans must learn to put more "peacock feathers into our business" because these people "not only admire splendor, they reverence it." "Mediterranean" peoples, he considered, lack "the sense of public navigation." And in Havana "they are children of pellucid chance . . . joyously irresponsible and incompetent."[30] Yet his playet *The Blood of the Martyr* anticipates in intent (though not skill) the savage anti-imperialism of Mark Twain's "To the Person Sitting in Darkness."

It was in connection with this question, when the issue was tearing at the roots of the American conscience, and Americans were dividing angrily over whether to play the imperial game or not, that Crane expressed his ideal of courage in general. Americans were exercised about the Philippines and Britons about South Africa, and everybody saw the parallels. Crane heartily approved a British protest because there was in it no hint of the "Boston . . . Great Movement . . ." mood, and it would "get no extra British soldiers killed in the Transvaal. . . . There is no screaming. . . . Instead of being the letter of a fiery agitator, it is the letter of a saddened man":

It all plainly resolves itself to a nationalistic basis. One hardly knows how to state it. One has the burning wish for the quick success of the American arms in the Philippines. At the same time, one has a still more burning wish that the Filipinos shall see us as just men, willing, anxious to deal fairly, govern with studious equity; depart, if need be, with honor.

However, Mr. Watson failed to express that comic vanity which leads one to long that the enemy should know that one is an honorable man. It could not possibly be admitted as necessary, but still Mr. Watson does not send any statement to the Boers assuring them that the English are honorable men. The feeling is certain to have been in Mr. Watson's bosom, but he said nothing. In these immense things one may have to watch the revolving of ponderous wheels with respect. A socialist cannot be sure what is best for the world at the moment as a paregoric, as a sleeping powder or as a disinfectant.[31]

What became essential to intelligence, Crane thought, was avoidance of that "comic vanity" in all its forms; yet avoidance was only relatively possible. Man was trapped in fate, nature, society, ignorance, and the partial rules of things. Of symbolic Private Nolan, Crane wrote: "Maybe someday, in a fairer, squarer land, he'll get his picture in the paper, too."[32] But for now he is non-respectable, nobody. On the other hand, "When a man is respectable, he is fettered to certain wheels, and when the chariot of fashion moves, he is dragged along at the rear. For his agony, he can console himself with the law that if a certain thing has not yet been respectable, he need only wait a sufficient time and it will eventually be so. The only disadvantage is that he is obliged to wait until other people wish to do it, and he is likely to lose his own craving."[33]

Convention generally was as inherently foolish as Cuban courting customs. Men and women everywhere seek, find, and love. And all the "barbed wire entanglements . . . and all the circumlocution and bulwarks and clever football interference and trouble and delay and protracted agony and duenas count for nothing, count for nothing against the tides of human life, which are in Cuba or Omaha controlled by the same moon."[34]

It had long been conventional for romantic artists to be anticonventional and put their trust in the tides of that "same moon" in Nature. Vigorous by conviction as by habit, sports-loving Crane adored the open air and knew his own mystique of nature. It is merely notorious, however, that the belief that "Nature never did betray the heart that loved her" moved Crane to black derision. A sad, even silent, anticonventionality was a stalwart part of his faith. "The lives of some people are one long apology. Mine was, once, but not now," he informed Nellie Crouse. "I go through the world unexplained, I suppose." And again, "You have no idea how it simplifies matters."[35] But it was no primal sanity of natural simplicity he sought—like Whitman or Thoreau. He did not believe in it and never knew it.

" 'The Sense of a City is War,' " said Crane, naming a picture in Linson's studio.[36] And he expanded the idea in an early sketch portraying how at first the stillness of the gold and green countryside seemed "incredibly monotonous" to vacationing city dwellers, "to the warriors from the metropolis. The sense of a city is battle." At length, however, "the song of the universal religion, the mighty mystic hymn of nature," silenced them with a comprehension of "the sacrilege of speech."[37] This matches the fine lantern-light on the water poem from *War Is Kind* where the "chorus of colors" confirms the music of the stars:

> Small glowing pebbles
> Thrown on the dark plane of evening
> Sing good ballads of God. . . .[38]

More often nature is ominous. In Mexico, ". . . no one feels like talking in the presence of these mountains that stand like gods on the world, for fear that they might hear."[39] Frequently Crane sees nature as terrible—as to the Nebraska farmers, or the streets of Fort Romper, or to the drowning sailor. War rages there, too. But, as almost everyone has agreed, and as the correspondent in "The Open Boat" perceives, in Crane nature is "flatly indifferent." And when a man knows that and "the pathos of his situation," he has, given the conditions of all the rest of his situation, only courage left—and irony.

VI

Irony is not an idea but a tactic. It is a way of taking the world slantwise, on the flank. It is probably necessary to suppose that the ironic capacity, in any of its modes, is temperamental. Temper informs the ironist's ideas and edges them. It is lucky if it be not wounded itself by them and goaded to despair. Some ironists keep sanguinely balanced like Franklin, some preserve sanctuaries of hope like Howells, some go down like Twain or Henry Adams. Along with his other gifts, a striking fact about Crane is his possession of an irony so powerful, so deep, and so his own at an age so young.

No one should suppose that an artist and critic of life and self so sensitive as Crane was ignorant of how thoroughly irony pervaded both explicitly his logical and implicitly his imaginative expression. In the tale, "His Majestic Lie," of a young American spy who sneaks back to Havana, risking death by torture (as Crane had more remotely done by infiltrating Havana as a correspondent before the occupation), Crane might almost have been defining himself in the character of the hero:

Johnnie was a typical American . . . a young man of great energy, ready to accomplish a colossal thing for the basic reason that he was ignorant of its magnitude. In fact he attacked all obstacles in life in a spirit of contempt, seeing them smaller than they were until he had actually surmounted them—when he was likely to be immensely pleased with himself. Somewhere in him there was a sentimental tenderness, but it was like a light seen afar at night; it came, went, appeared again in a new place, flickered, flared, went out, left you in a void and angry. And if his sentimental tenderness was a light, the darkness in which it puzzled you was his irony of soul. This irony was directed first at himself; then at you; then at the nation and the flag; then at God. It was a midnight in which you searched for the little elusive, ashamed spark of tender sentiment. Sometimes you thought this was all pretext, the manner and the way of fear of the wit of others; sometimes you thought he was a hardened savage; usually you did not think, but waited in the cheerful certainty that in time the little flare of light would appear in the gloom.[40]

Applied strictly to Crane, however, the "directions" of the irony would have to be revised somewhat. His ironies (for they were various) were directed first at himself; then at you; then at the nation and the flag—and at all abstract conventions and pomposities; then at God; then at Man; and finally back at himself again. The ultimate stretch of Crane's irony was its enabling him to revolt against his own revolt—because that, too, was based on vanity.

"Vanity of vanities, all is vanity, saith the Preacher," in that most ironic of books. The sense of the word there is, of course, its root meaning of "emptiness." But Crane would have applied it in both that and its modern sense of "conceit." He saw it everywhere and derided it. In himself: "When I reached twenty-one years and first really scanned my personal egotism I was fairly dazzled by the size of it," he wrote Nellie Crouse. "The Matterhorn could be no more than a tenpin to it."[41]

And he remarked it in others repeatedly as he investigated life. The poor had it. His story "An Experiment in Misery" had shown that not only "cowardice" but "their present state of conceit" damned Bowery folk. "A person who thinks himself superior to the rest of us because he has no job and no pride and no clean clothes [had that at one point been Stephen Crane?] is as badly conceited as Lillian Russell."[42] But the matching piece, "An Experiment in Luxury," told a still more damning tale of the rich. It was a lie that the very rich were miserable; they lived in a beauty and freedom as well as comfort and security unknown to the squalid. And they were not responsible for the difference: "Nobody is responsible for anything. I wish to Heaven somebody was, and then we could all jump on him. . . ." The experimenter is made to feel that "all this had merely happened; the great secret hand had guided them here and had guided others there. The eternal mystery of social condition exasperated him at this time. He wondered if incomprehensible justice were the sister of open wrong."

But the discovery of this experiment is that princely luxury delivers itself at last into vicious but dreary sins of pride. It all came to center in "The Gold Woman," the society matron, the "dragon," of joyless, "terrible pride," with the face of "a grim old fighter . . . for place before the white altars of social excellence." There "was the true abode of conservatism—in the mothers"—savage chieftainesses—"controlled" by "tradition and superstition" who "respected themselves with a magnitude of respect heaven seldom allows on earth." Yet luxury was pleasant. If the rich "were fairly virtuous," he concluded, the experimenter "could see no reason why they should be so persistently pitied. And no doubt they would dispense their dollars like little seeds upon the soil of the world if it were not for the fact that since the days of the ancient great political economist, the more exalted forms of virtue have grown to be utterly impracticable."[43]

Like the works of the great realists, Crane's are often studies in vision, in discovery, in revelation. And a critique which studied them as exercises in the uneditorialized revelation of human vanity, its consequences, and its meaning would return major rewards in fresh, deep understanding.

For the ultimate twist of Crane's irony came from his perception that man's ridiculous, wicked conceit was necessary to his existence in nature and society. In "The Blue Hotel," because the idea is not the point of the story (though it is necessary to a grasp of the point) and the economy of the short story was pressing him, Crane permitted himself an authorial intrusion. Flushed with hubris, the Swede leaves the hotel, stepping out into the symbolic rage of the blizzard from which he will take refuge in the saloon where he will be murdered. In the midst of the tempest, Crane commented, "One viewed the existence of man as a marvel, and conceded a glamor of wonder to these lice which were caused to cling to a whirling, fire-smitten, ice-locked, disease-stricken, space-lost bulb. The conceit of man was explained by this storm to be the very engine of life. One was a coxcomb not to die in it."

And the same was true of man in society. Crane in 1894 grasped the same sense of the raucous fun of slum-life which Howells had registered in A Hazard of New Fortunes. They were forgetting death, Howells suggested. Riding home in the cars from Coney Island with the drunk and rowdy, Crane imagined himself in converse with a "Philosopher" who commented on the scene: "I see revealed more clearly the purposes of the inexorable universe which plans to amuse us occasionally to keep us from the rebellion of suicide. And I see how simply and drolly it accomplishes its end. The insertion of a mild quantity of the egotism of sin into the minds of these young men causes them to wildly enjoy themselves. . . . This return of the people to their battles always has a stupendous effect upon me . . . the gaiety which arises upon these Sunday night occasions . . . [has] an unspeakable air of recklessness and bravado and grief about it. . . . You can hear the undercurrent of it in that song, which is really as grievous as the cry of a child. If he had no vanity—well, it is fortunate for the world that we are not all great thinkers."[44]

If man's vanity was absurd, it was also necessary—and therefore tragic. And it ended finally in mystery for Crane. He had nothing at all of that smug confidence about summing up the universe in neat formulae eventually available to every schoolboy which characterized the popular scientism—and some of the serious science and philosophy—of the day. On the contrary, much of Crane's most intimate expression, particularly his religious poetry, suggests that, for all the mind of man can tell, God, intentionally or not, is playing games with us. The suggestion of King Lear is not out of keeping.

One of the missed opportunities of American intellectual life in the latter nineteenth century, as Herbert W. Schneider pointed out some years ago, was the chance Darwinism afforded theologians to construct a new Calvinism. Edwards had done it after deism; the neo-orthodox would do it after Freud. Perhaps Kierkegaard did it for his age—but he was unknown in this country. Temperamentally and imaginatively—though not of course theologically—Crane expressed that possibility in his art and view. In the end, what one means by his irony is that, while Crane was sometimes a romantic, an adventurous boy, he was also a tough-minded realist with a tragic vision more Calvinistic, in its perceptions of the blasphemy as well as the necessity of man's conceit, than naturalistic. He guessed at an ultimate war with God. And he had a nearly Kierkegaardian sense of the ridiculousness of the situation. He could not finally take himself or man seriously in realistic, tragic, naturalistic, Calvinistic, nor, of course, neo-romantic perspectives.

The last irony was directed even against Crane's own moral fight. Then, as in the most moving of Crane's personal documents, his letters to Nellie Crouse, it made him one with Shakespeare, Melville, and Clemens. "The final wall of the wise man's thought . . . ," he concluded, "is Human Kindness"—and then, with a last self-deprecation, "of course." Christian gentlemen *manqué*, he was in as thorough revolt against respectablility and moralism as Henry James, Sr., but without that philosopher's counterillumination. He groped for an absolute vision. He would have settled for a piety and morality of pity, sympathy, of open humanity. But he was not sure. At twenty-eight Crane died in the heroic but painful condition of soul Keats diagnosed in Shakespeare as "negative capability."

CHAPTER 5

Crane's Art before
The Red Badge of Courage

I

W. D. HOWELLS always refused to consider that *The Red Badge* was Crane's masterpiece. He liked *Maggie* better. He liked the tough-minded, clear-sighted, disillusioned investigator who saw through conventions and sentimentalities to the facts of social war and was solicitous of its victims. He hoped Crane would outgrow playing with soldiers and black-rider wars with heaven. Howells knew about the early conversion of Crane's literary ideal from Kipling to Howells's realism. He sensed the tentativeness of that conversion. There remained Crane's constant temptations toward neo-romanticism, at least of a Rooseveltian stripe. And there was that "secret" which Howells saw in Crane, the unfathomable something which held him convinced that war everywhere—with God, nature, men, and self—was the irreducible, tragic condition of man.

In short, the Crane who learned what he had to know before he could write *The Red Badge* was multivalent. He had an ideal of realism which had supplanted but not suppressed a boyish ideal of romance. And he had a self which could not be contained in either camp, which has always successfully eluded categorization, and which broke out in unpremeditated, startling verse at the first peak of his creative powers.

Multivalence accounts for his ability to produce *Sullivan County Sketches* at the same time as he was struggling toward the first printed *Maggie* and the half-realized "Midnight Sketches." In the admirable introduction to Melvin Schoberlin's edition of *The Sullivan County Sketches* (1949)—which was to have accompanied his not yet published definitive life of Crane—the key to the situa-

100

tion first appeared. Writing to Lily Brandon Munroe, Crane confided that he had "renounced the clever school in literature" and
"my clever Rudyard Kipling style" for a creed

. . . identical with the one of Howells and Garland and in this way I
became involved in the beautiful war between those who say that art is
man's substitute for nature and we are the most successful in art when we
approach the nearest to nature and truth, and those who say—well, I don't
know what they say. Than that they can't say much but they fight
villainously and keep Garland and I out of the big magazines. . . . The
two years of fighting have been well-spent. . . . They used to call me "that
terrible, young radical," but now they are beginning to hem and haw and
smile—those very old coons who used to adopt a condescending air toward
me. There is an irony in the present situation that I enjoy, devil take them
for a parcel of old, cringing, conventionalized hens.[1]

There had been little to flutter the "hens" about the Sullivan
sketches, however, except perhaps a youthful exuberance in the
author. If there were, as Schoberlin justly says, signs of Stephen
Crane emerging from the chrysalis, the sketches belonged to an ancient tradition of American sporting, out-of-doors, masculine
humor—what is often loosely called "frontier" humor with its established techniques of slapstick, burlesque, and "the sell." Before
Crane's running afoul of the sloppy parade of the Junior Order of
American Mechanics in his Asbury Park correspondence and embarrassing Whitelaw Reid politically, the *New York Tribune* had
printed five sketches, one each Sunday, in July 1892. After that the
Cosmopolitan, perhaps in reaction against Howells who had ex-
plosively ceased to be its editor on June 30, bought one.

Less filled with "clever and witty expedients" than Crane supposed, his sketches foreshadowed greatness. Perhaps the most wholly successful is the one without slapstick: "Killing His Bear, a
Winter Tragedy with Three Actors"—the bear, a hound, and "the
little man." In the frozen woods the man waits. "On the ridge-top a
dismal choir of hemlocks crooned over one that had fallen. The dying sun created a dim purple and flame-colored tumult on the
horizon's edge. . . . A gray, ponderous stillness came heavily in the
steps of the sun." And on the stillness broke the belling of the dog:
"a hound, as he nears large game, has the griefs of the world on his
shoulders, and his baying tells of the approach of death. He is sorry
he came." When the man "saw swirling fur over his gun barrel,"
tumult and stillness were both his part:

The earth faded to nothing. Only space and the game, the aim and the hunter. Mad emotions, powerful to rock worlds, hurled through the little man, but did not shake his tiniest nerve.

When the rifle cracked, it shook his soul to a profound depth. Creation rocked and the bear stumbled.

Thus far, that is not unworthy of Faulkner or Hemingway in the same vein. But Crane was unable to rest in the romanticism either of them would have left dominating the sketch. He had to undercut it. Scrambling on the bear's trail, Crane's little man leaps for joy when he finds it dead, ". . . waving his hat as if he were leading the cheering of thousands. He ran up and kicked the ribs of the bear. Upon his face was the smile of the successful lover."

That same as yet slightly unfocused irony applies to the "clever Rudyard-Kipling style" of the sketches. It is a burlesque tone—the high style mocking low matter. In "The Octopush," for example, a drunken guide leaves four fishermen marooned on stumps in a lake:

A ghostlike mist came and hung upon the waters. The pond became a graveyard. The gray tree trunks and dark logs turned to monuments and crypts. Fireflies were wisp-lights dancing over graves, and then, taking regular shapes, appeared like brass nails in crude caskets. The [guide] . . . began to gibber. A gibber in a bass voice appalls the stoutest heart. It is the declamation of a genie. The little man began to sob; another groaned; and the two remaining, being timid by nature, swore great lurid oaths which blazed against the sky.

This easily became pseudo-biblical as well as pulpiteering and mock - William Jennings Bryan. When the guide did come near, "The little man kicked him. But the others cried out against him, so directly he left off." At its worst it could grate terribly on the ears, as in "The Cry of a Huckleberry Pudding," where the little man's stomach-ache incites "a howl that rolled and pealed. . . . It clamored like a song of forgotten war, and died away to the screams of a maiden. The pleadings of fire-surrounded children mingled with the calls of wave-threatened sailors. Two barbarian tribes clashed together on a sunburnt plain; a score of barekneed clansmen crossed claymores amid gray rocks; a woman saw a lover fall; a dog was stabbed in an alley; a steel knight bit dust with bloody mouth. . . ."

Crane, hurried, distracted, or tired, would always be in danger of lapsing back toward that pompous style. It was a danger inherent in the conflict between his heroics and his irony. His intensity, as he well knew, was liable to bathos. The careful student of the sources of his style will need to look to *The Bible*, to the schoolroom classics, and to pulpit style as well as to Kipling. But he would do well also to study the prevailing tones of the sports pages and of humor magazines like *Judge*, *Life* and *Puck*.

The largest significance of *The Sullivan County Sketches* may be, however, their recording so early and purely the meaning and weight to Crane the artist of the experience of Crane the sportsman. As we have seen, Crane from boyhood joined the sporting fraternity with "fiendish glee." He rode, hiked, hunted and camped, played baseball with a sacrificial passion, coached and played a bantam quarterback on a Jersey town football team in the fearsome days of massed interference and helping the runner. He pursued the mystery of manliness into the West as far as Mexico, on the filibuster *Commodore*, to Greece, and at last to Cuba.

It might be arguable that the trope basic to Crane's vision was that of the game. But the complexities of that vision to which he wished so desperately to be faithful were, to use one of his favorite words, immense. The trope is pervasive. He begins his serious efforts at fiction with hunting and camping sketches. The opening scene—and a governing symbol—of *Maggie* shows slum children viciously playing a favorite game: "King of the Hill." No few poems suggest that the procession of life is a game God plays with man, keeping the rules to Himself. The psychology, the whole essence of *The Red Badge of Courage*, Crane said he learned on the football field. As soon as he got to Greece and into combat he rejoiced that *The Red Badge* was all right—the "mental attitude" was right. And the war Crane saw was, repeatedly, "A Game"—as were his visions of *la hora de la verdad* in the West, Mexico, and Cuba.

For many reasons, however, the simpler ones being social, Crane was no Wister, Remington, nor Roosevelt. His vision was not only darker but deeper. Where they saw pain, struggle, and victory he saw agony and despair—at best tragedy. And above all, he saw irony. That irony could be wonderfully funny. One wonders why it is so seldom noticed, for instance, that "The Bride Comes to Yellow Sky" is a hilariously funny parody of neo-romantic lamentations over "The Passing of the West." The last marshal, tamed by a prosaic marriage, is exempted from playing the Game so absurdly romanticized by Street and Smith, the *Police Gazette*, and finally Owen Wister. His occupation gone, the last Bad Man, a part-time worker anyhow, shuffles off into the sunset dragging boot tracks through the dust like the tracks of the last dinosaur.

His experience of sports brought Crane knowledge, and attitudes consequent on that knowledge, important to his point of view. It gave him the experience of testing his courage and thence his personal knowledge of pain and fear, victory and defeat. From that vantage point he commanded the cosmic gambler's stoic outlook: despising the petty, safe, and comfortable; prizing the chance-taking, the enterprising, the seeking, aggressive and tough. In this respect he was at one with the prophets of the strenuous life.[2] But he went beyond them in the depth of his forceful but ambivalent compassion for losers. He was anxious that their courage or at least their agony be defended against and registered upon the smug and ignorant. But he would not defend them against the law, against the rules of the game of life. It is because they express that compassion so magnificently, each differently from the other, that "The Open Boat" and "The Blue Hotel" are superior to, for instance, "Five White Mice," "A Man and Some Others," or "Horses—One Dash."

II

Whatever else it may be in actuality, *Maggie: A Girl of the Streets*, was intended to be—and was understood by Crane to be—a work of realism. "I had no other purpose in writing 'Maggie' than to show people to people as they seem to me," he wrote in his oft-quoted letter to Miss Catherine Harris. "If that be evil, make the most of it."[3] This reflected Howells's definition of realism as "the truthful treatment of material" which Crane had picked up from Garland in 1891 and with which his post-Kipling creed was "identical." They all insisted that it did not mean being "photographic" but only, as Crane explained Garland explaining Howells, that "the novelist be true to himself and to things as he sees them."[4]

Crane's unspoken pact with Howells was the same Howells had with all the innumerable writers he helped. No discipleship was required, only honest development. Both sides were free to disagree without penalty so long as the amenities were observed, and between Howells and Crane they always were.[5] Crane grasped the essence of the idea of realism from the start in holding it to be a matter of seeing, a question of vision. In repeatedly stressing vision in moments of self-analysis, he proclaimed his continuous adherence to the doctrine. Late in 1894, after *The Red Badge* had been written, Howells helped relieve Crane's poverty with a rare interview. Crane rewarded him with a presentation so almost uniquely clear among Howells's many explanations of realism that it becomes a major document. Presumably Crane contributed substantially to it.

Howells has been speaking of the "problem novel" and advising confinement of preaching to the pulpit. He continues:

"But it is the business of the novel—"

"Ah!" said the other man.

"It is the business of the novel to picture the daily life in the most exact terms possible, with an absolute and clear sense of proportion. That is the important matter—the proportion. As a usual thing, I think, people have absolutely no sense of proportion. Their noses are tight against life, you see. They perceive mountains where there are no mountains, but frequently a great peak appears no larger than a rat trap. An artist sees a dog down the street—well, his eye instantly relates the dog to its surroundings. The dog is proportioned to the buildings and the trees. Whereas, many people can conceive of that dog's tail resting upon a hilltop."

"You have often said that the novel is a perspective," observed the other man.

"A perspective, certainly. It is a perspective made for the benefit of people who have no true use of their eyes. The novel, in its real meaning, adjusts the proportions. It preserves the balances. It is in this way that lessons are to be taught and reforms to be won. When people are introduced to each other they will see the resemblances, and won't want to fight so badly."

"I suppose that when a man tries to write 'what the people want'—when he tries to reflect the popular desire, it is a bad quarter of an hour for the laws of proportion."[6]

Supposing, as there is fair warrant for doing, that *Maggie* went through several drafts (Stallman guessed at four),[7] it is clear that the turn toward realism is what differentiates it from *The Sullivan County Sketches* both in style and "perspective." Perhaps Crane referred to that change in his inscription to Howells of "the veneration and gratitude of Stephen Crane for many things he has learned of the common man and, above all, for a certain readjustment of his point of view victoriously concluded some time in 1892." With "point of view," the context becomes almost saturated with the realists' conjuring words.

Maggie: A Girl of the Streets is, then, a Bowery "perspective made for the benefit of people who have no true use of their eyes."

And that seems the key to settling the problem of its "form." Formally Crane's problem was a characteristically realistic or, indeed, Jamesian problem of perspective and proportion, of vision; and he solved it as well as he was able by the characteristic technique James called "scenes" and "pictures," habitually setting the action within the picture. Crane's numbered sections are significant of this technique, each having a kind of unity of its own. With his characteristic intensity, indeed, Crane may have scored an advance on realistic painterlike technique. Reviewing the 1896 Appleton edition of *Maggie,* Frank Norris's quick, seeking eye spotted something in "the way Mr. Crane tells his story. The picture he makes is not a simple carefully composed painting, serious, finished, scrupulously studied, but rather scores and scores of tiny flashlight photographs, instantaneous, caught as it were, on the run."[8] Though Norris did not, I think, grasp the larger structure and was, as reviewers often must be, wrong about other things, that one insight was acute, brilliant to the point of standing to this day ahead of most *Maggie* criticism.

But the date of Norris's comment brings us to a point upon which all comment on *Maggie* must now pivot. For most purposes, especially the critical, a revolution took place in 1966. One does not read Norris's bowdlerized Appleton edition of 1896, though it reigned thereafter for seventy years. One reads the Crane edition of 1893, the one privately printed, so rare the *Crane Newsletter* undertook to print a census of known copies, the scandalous failure which was and is a great book.

The honor and glory of making that revolution appear to belong about equally to Professors Maurice Bassan, whose *Maggie* "casebook" uses Crane's own edition conjoined with fine critical source material like Norris's review, and Joseph Katz, whose facsimile[9] edition begins with a magisterial introduction. Both volumes are of the same year, and there is honor aplenty for them to share, even in alphabetical order. They have had flattering followers, and the copy-text of the *Virginia Edition* thereafter became the 1893 *Maggie*.

As Norris was quick to point out in 1896, fiction about ruined prostitutes and "the life of the mean streets of a great city" was old stuff. Unique style and method put Stephen Crane's work "out of the ordinary." But Norris worked from a text which Appleton wanted to ride on the fame of *The Red Badge* and required Crane to clean up. I see no escape from admitting that Howells must have been right when he tried in July 1896 to launch Crane together with the first Jewish-American novelist Abraham Cahan in the *New York World* with a piece done in his very best manner and called "New York Low Life in Fiction." He had succeeded with Paul Laurence Dunbar only the month before. Now he invoked the charms of Benjamin A. Baker and Edward Harrigan's madly popular Irish "b'hoy" comedies, of the new Yiddish theater as he had begun to know it, of "Chimmie Fadden" and everybody else who was, as he said, "known earlier" where Crane was "first in the field." I do not think better criticism of *Maggie* has been written yet. Howells did not let himself say, as he had in *Harper's Weekly* a year earlier, that *Maggie* as he had read it was not going to get published because of "the impossibility to cultured ears of a parlance whose texture is so largely profanity." But though now he called it "the finest art" and Greek-like,[10] he did not get it published.

What was so impossible about the language in *Maggie?* It is not easy now to tell, yet Hemingway before World War II never dared what Crane dared, fatally, in 1893. A quick census of profanities (there are no obscenities) in *Maggie* rather daunts one by the fact of their simple innocence. Not counting allusions to bad words ("oath," "curse," "swear," etc.), in *Maggie* they say "hell" separately and in various combinations about ninety-six times; "damn," with "damned," scores sixty-four; the name of the deity (spelled "Gawd") is taken in vain nine times; "devil" is spoken eleven times. That is about it—among something like 20,000 words. Though it's embarrassing that Stephen Crane should have walked in the slush with broken shoes, nearly starving, on account of that record of dialect, it is probably true that, in recovering a profanity so common most present readers would hardly catch it, one recovers the key, from the 1893 edition, to *Maggie*. The ordinary little adjuration, not comic but fateful because the date was 1893, is, "Go teh hell!"

It helps from the start to see that Crane gave *Maggie* an almost unmistakable, nearly perfect structure. For the benefit of a Voice of America audience I once dealt with that structure in detail.[11] Perhaps here we need only remember that the structure is built of four elements: "A," "B," "C," and "D." The first begins with the childhood of Maggie, her tough, fighting brother Jimmie, and the baby Tommie. The perspective presents a sort of moral ecology of Rum Alley and the slums. It shows the children living in a state of social and familial war, with their survival in doubt. By the end of "A," the alcoholic father has been murdered by the mother in a drunken family brawl. Tommie has died and been sentimentally buried. Jimmy, on the streets, has grown leather hard in violence, egotism, and vice. Mother Mary has become a hideous alcoholic public-court dragon. But Maggie has become a flower that "blossomed in a mud puddle . . . a most rare and wonderful production of a tenement district, a pretty girl." More wonderfully still, she is innocent. It was Crane's *donnée*. Nevertheless, in that Section V, which modulates from "A" to "B," Jimmie says, "Mag, I'll tell yeh dis! See? Yeh've edder got teh go teh hell or go teh work."

We have entered "B" when Maggie goes to work in a sweatshop and Jimmie brings home his pal, bartender Pete. Pete observes, "Say, Mag, I'm stuck on yer shape. It's outa sight." Thus he becomes the wooing knight of her dreams. Meanwhile, Mary ever more violently deteriorates. And "B" develops, descending, scene and picture, until Mary, smashing the furniture and losing her inevitable fight with Jimmie, tells Maggie,

> "Damn yeh, git out! . . .
> Go teh hell an' good riddance."
> She went.

That leads to the scene of one of the best bar-fights in literature. Everything leads to Pete's seduction, desertion, and rejection of Maggie. When she tries to come back home, a suddenly high-principled Pharisee and his mother laugh and jeer her to scorn and turn her out. When she goes to Pete, reminding him of promises, he is deaf. When she asks, "But where kin I go?" one knows what Pete will cry out: "Oh, go teh hell."

On the street she then makes two discoveries: first, that ". . . men looked at her with calculating eyes." But then she glimpses a hope, a clerical-looking "stout gentleman in a silk hat and a chaste black coat," most decorously buttoned—perhaps a bishop:

The girl had heard of the Grace of God and she decided to approach this man.

His beaming, chubby face was a picture of benevolence and kind-heartedness. His eyes shone good-will.

But as the girl timidly accosted him, he gave a convulsive moment and saved his respectability by a vigorous sidestep. He did not risk it to save a soul. For how was he to know that there was a soul before him that needed saving?

If anything in muscular Christianity had been lost on the good man, it was demonstratedly not muscle. And so ends "B."

Part "C" consists of one short, controversial chapter about which my perceptions have changed—though not exactly in the ways sometimes alleged by commentators—since 1960. For this crucial Chapter XVII Crane reverted to what has been said to have been the earliest state of the novel, when nobody had a name. Here Maggie becomes just "a girl of the painted cohorts of the city," well dressed, well shod, dainty, and expertly soliciting. In swiftly telescoped moments she steps down and down through the social strata of the city—compressing perhaps years as she passes. James D. McCabe in *New York by Sunlight and Gaslight*, 1882, estimated that it took a girl five to seven years to fall from the fashionable "first-class houses" down the scales to waterfront degradation and death by disease, brutality, or the river. This girl steps across "glittering avenues" in one paragraph to "the restless doors of saloons" in the next. Then she begins a series of cinematically fast-paced symbolic encounters. A *boulevardier* turns her down because she is "neither new, Parisian, nor theatrical." In swift succession she is rebuffed by respectable, middle-class, and laboring men, a boy, a drunk—always descending. At last there came "a man with blotched features" who claims to have a date, then "a ragged being with shifting, blood-shot eyes," dirty hands, and no money.

When "almost to the river" she encounters the last customer, the one Professor Bowers excised from the text in the *Virginia Edition* for esthetic reasons:

. . . a huge fat man in torn and greasy garments. His grey hair straggled down over his forehead. His small, bleared eyes, sparkling from amidst great rolls of red fat, swept eagerly over the girl's upturned face. He laughed, his brown, disordered teeth gleaming under a grey, grizzled moustache from which beer-drops dripped. His whole body gently quivered and shook like that of a dead jelly fish. Chuckling and leering, he followed the girl of the crimson legions.

After that there is nothing at all in Chapter XVIII, part "C," except the final paragraph:

At their feet the river appeared a deathly black hue. Some hidden factory sent up a yellow glare, that lit for a moment the waters lapping oilily against timbers. The various sounds of life, made joyous by distance and seeming unapproachableness, came faintly and died away to a silence.

No more of Maggie Johnson. It used to seem to me that the sudden shift in method, from the dramatic vitality and the solidity of specification of "B" to the symbolism and imagism of "C," was an artistic lapse in the architectonics of the novel. The mere brevity of the element, made briefer and more lightweight by omitting the horrible last man, placed Crane as artist in danger of bathos—achieving anticlimax where climax must be. If one assumes that indeed "C" is meant for climax, that the succeeding "D" element is the Aristotelian anticlimax, or deliberate relaxation from tragic climax, "C" remains too brief, too light, too tonally wrong, too riskily close to bathos. Frank Norris, in his review, registered his sense of the point in saying that "the downfall of Maggie, the motif of the tale, strikes one as handled in a manner almost too flippant for the seriousness of the subject."

Exactly there, however, I, like Norris, went wrong in reading the novel. "The motif of the tale," is not, all evidence to the contrary notwithstanding, the personal history of Maggie Johnson. The motif of the tale is what the story of a girl of the streets means. And the tragic climax, which is also the normal climax of the realistic novel, is revelation. The revelation—of the truth—the teaching of people who see falsely how to use their eyes aright, comes in "D" and climaxes in powerful tragic irony with the last words of the novel. What the artist.had to get done, and what saves "C" and justifies its whole existence as Crane wrote it, is to kill off Maggie effectively, so as to establish the grounds for the climax. "C," then, is preclimactic, not weak climax, and it is sufficient if not brilliant in performing its function. It shows that Crane's prentice hand had mastered certain difficult tricks of the trade.

The last section, with tragic force, creates a work finer than even Bernard Berenson, an admirer of Crane, saw in *Maggie*: a "fairly accurate picture of Irish slums in New York, done with economy, precision, and no little art in presentation."[12] In moral perspective, "D" stands for shattering ironic demolition of the characters, the circumstances, and so the civilization, the popular sentimentalities, and the respectable hypocrisies responsible for snuffing out a girl. Jimmie comes home and says flatly, "Well, Mag's dead," while Mary gnaws at her bread. The last of Pete shows him braying drunkenly, "I'm damn good' f'ler and w'en anyone trea's me ri', I treats zem ri'! Shee!" while smart little whores, working at the saloon stratum of the life, mockingly fleece him. But the last irony results from a conflict in perspectives set up between the pathos of Maggie the victim and the terror inspired by our last sight of Mary, mother of destruction.

Crane's *donnée,* once more, was that Maggie "blossomed in a mud puddle." That central metaphor raises the question whether the story is about the flower or the puddle, from which every frog tells Maggie, "Go teh hell." Certainly the reader comes to know more about the puddle than about its impossible flower. The story tells, as Crane said variously in various inscriptions upon the original printing, that "environment may be a tremendous thing in life" and that therefore there may be "room in heaven even for an occasional street-girl." Nevertheless the book establishes unmistakably the point that his environmental concern, common to the realistic tradition at least since Flaubert and Turgenev, by no means prepared him or his work to abandon the idea of personal moral responsibility and guilt. On the contrary, in the tension lay much of the essential irony.

The right question becomes whether the motif of the tale is not actually perception of the ironies upon which the dynamics of the work climax with fearful emphasis. Though they are indeed the old tragic ironies of the clash between illusion and reality, Crane's art, especially in his portrait of Mary Johnson, her character and behavior as mother and moralist, suggests that *Maggie*'s motif is at last the shame, sin, and horror of conventional condemnations of the prostitute, the "wicked" or "fallen" woman.

Crane's was, of course, no new theme. Don't you think, an interviewer asked Howells, that women are more compassionate toward the sins of others than men?

"Ye-es", drawled Crane's friend, "more compassionate—toward—the sins— —of *men.*"

Thomas Bailey Aldrich, however, gives us a perfect example of the sort of hypocritical sentimentality Crane set out to smash:

ANDROMEDA
The smooth-worn coin and threadbare classic phrase
Of Grecian myths that did beguile my youth,
Beguile me not as in the olden days:
I think more grief and beauty dwell with truth.

Andromeda, in fetters by the sea,
Star-pale with anguish till young Perseus came,
Less moves me with her suffering than she,
The slim girl figure fettered to dark shame,
That nightly haunts the park, there, like a shade,
Trailing her wretchedness from street to street.
See where she passes—neither wife nor maid.
How all mere fiction crumbles at her feet!
Here is woe's self, and not the mask of woe:
A legend's shadow shall not move you so!

Against that as well as the Peck family's thunders of eternal per-
dition, Stephen set the climax of *Maggie*. That last chapter has no
competition I can recall. Jimmie has brought the news: " 'Mag's
dead.' 'Deh hell she is,' said the woman. She continued her meal.
When she finished her coffee she began to weep."

Neighbor women gather for the emotional jag of the wake. Part
of the melodrama shall be that Mary must "fergive" Maggie. Well
fortified with her snack, Mary puts on a fine performance:

"Yeh'll fergive her, Mary!" pleaded the woman in black. The mourner
essayed to speak but her voice gave way. She shook her great shoulders
frantically, in an agony of grief. Hot tears seemed to scald her quivering
face. Finally her voice came and arose like a scream of pain.
"Oh, yes, I'll fergive her! I'll fergive her!"

That climax confirms *Maggie* as a book about moral ecology, the
real meaning of the slums, the effect of the puddle on its flower.
The book is as nearly Ibsenian as anything. That last screech lets the
cutting edge fall just where it must, where, in climax, the entire
narrative structure insists. And so the narrative structure is justified
in artistic fulfillment. In the last artful lines the narrative, the scenes
and pictures (including "C"), and several lesser lines of irony join in
that tragic irony which induced Howells to think of Sophocles.

In his tragic irony Crane found an angle of moral attack so
crushing that his dedicatory inscriptions reveal themselves to be
quiet sarcasms—laconic. No one who responded to the blow against
convention and sentimentality which weighted his structure to fall
in climax upon the awesome hypocrisy of the dreadful mother
would miss his point. What could he have said to the rest?

With our present revival (after a fleeting illusion that it was
withering away) of the American slum in more ominous, less trac-

table forms, *Maggie* has become more contemporary to us, speaks more immediately to our condition, than many a book written on like themes during the current century and thought somehow "more modern."

In that light of immediacy, one comes to feel that the ancient matter of evolutionary literary history—the problem of the sources in Crane's reading of *Maggie*—does not really matter. Howells and Norris were right in thinking that Crane's vision and his technique were the important issues. Crane was right in his indignation at the presumption of social figures in England who enquired languidly about what French authors he had cribbed from. It is a nonquestion.

For a time it looked as if the late Professor Marston LaFrance were right in his observation of 1974 that the "school" of interpretation of Crane as a literary naturalist was largely "solemn nonsense" and that "sooner or later this school should have to close its doors to signify, at last, its critical bankruptcy."[13] Though I had made so bold in *The Light of Common Day* as to venture the opinion that in the strict sense there are in fact no American naturalists, I am not sure Donald Pizer is going to let us get away with that. But I still feel sure about Crane. In a series of essays climaxing in *The Novels of Theodore Dreiser* (1976), Pizer has been revising our previous ways of coming at naturalism. It is possible that I have not altogether understood Pizer, but I still feel sure about Crane. That final, impassable chasm remains. With Crane there can be no last analysis; he did not live long enough to commit himself intrinsically to any "ism." The only thing he said he was trying to become was "a realist." But he did not live to grow old enough to become an "ist." No "ism" in fact precipitated itself out of the alembic of his mind. He remains forever a Seeker, an apprentice to himself.

III

In fact, his next book, *The Black Riders*, immensely complicates the notion of any sort of settlement. It was wholly other than realistic, and the poems set Howells to grumbling about a waste of Crane's time and talents. It was free verse, strikingly imagistic, and masculine in a total rejection of Tennysonian euphonies. Perhaps it was symbolistic, perhaps not—it was hard to tell. Any reader could tell that the poet was earnestly engaged with ideas even if he did not know that the poet had insisted to the publisher that he not "cut all the ethical sense out of the book. All the anarchy, perhaps. It is the anarchy which I particularly insist upon. . . . The ones which refer to God . . . I am obliged to have. . . ."[14] Hoffman has summed up the sense of these key poems in his heading for a chapter interpreting them: "War in Heaven."

No naturalist, much less a "pure" one, could have taken the idea of the reality of God seriously. There is no doubt that Crane, while of several minds and consciously "anarchical" (the worst kind of revolutionary in the popular mind of the day), was serious. One critic has drawn extended parallels between *The Black Riders* and John Bunyan's masterpiece.[15] Young, semi-educated, a preacher's son, and unaccustomed to discussing ideas, Crane doubtless exaggerated the "anarchy" of his position. Indeed, if he had been more *au courant*, he might have lapsed into the conspiracy of skeptical silence of the polite. As it was, he cared too much.

Except, as must always be the case with explications, for a wish to read some poems a little differently from the way he does, one can scarcely improve on Hoffman's "War in Heaven" chapter. It is in many ways the heart of his admirable achievement in *The Poetry of Stephen Crane*. The religious attitudes, and Hoffman's convincing inferences as to their provenience, of Crane's poems we have already summarized. But it may be useful to quote representatively.

Sometimes Crane imagined in accord with a naturalistic sense of reality:

LXVI

If I should cast off this tattered coat,
And go free into the mighty sky;
If I should find nothing there
But a vast blue,
Echoless, ignorant—
What then?

But again a truly Calvinistic imagination responds:

LXVIII

A spirit sped
Through spaces of night;
And as he sped, he called,
"God! God!"
He went through valleys
Of black death-slime,

Ever calling,
"God! God!"
Their echoes
From crevice and cavern
Mocked him:
"God! God! God!"
Fleetly into the plains of space
He went, ever calling,
"God! God!"
Eventually, then, he screamed,
Mad in denial,
"Ah, there is no God!"
A swift hand,
A sword from the sky,
Smote him,
And he was dead.

Crane had, however, no idea of being intimidated by that awful Jehovah. "Well, then, I hate Thee, unrighteous picture" (XII), he informed the Old Testament God who visited the sins of the fathers upon the heads of the children. But he also knew a "God of his inner thoughts" who

. . . looked at him
With soft eyes
Lit with infinite comprehension
And said, "My poor child!"

(LI)

For the blustering Bully Jehovah, he was quick to express contempt:

Withal there is One whom I fear;
I fear to see grief upon that face.
Perchance, friend, He is not your God;
If so, spit upon Him.
By it you will do no profanity.
But I—
Ah, sooner would I die
Than see tears in those eyes of my soul.

(LIII)

Though there was much in *The Black Riders* not dreamt of in the philosophy of *Le Roman expérimental,* or of *Criticism and Fiction,* that says nothing of the quality as poetry of these and the rest of Crane's "lines," "pills," or what not, as he called them to evade the sissy soubriquet of "poet." They constitute a perfectly personal expression, defying categorization; they are much more difficult to paraphrase than they seem until one tries; at their best, they are extraordinarily subtle in phonetic effect. One can find analogues, but no true sources for them as poems. To be sure they are "biblical" and have predecessors in the wisdom literature of the ages—or the pseudowisdom literature of Crane's age. But there are no poems like these: Crane, by not trying to be a poet, achieved a genuinely organic expression of the religious, moral, amatory, the nature-loving, and particularly the ironic experiences rioting through his head.

The result was above all intense. Taking the best of Crane's poetry from all volumes (and one judges poets first and last by their best), the imagery is unforgettable. The power of definition is as illuminating as Emily Dickinson's. The sharp, often agonizingly ironic parables are dramatic, with a symbolism often almost surrealistically extreme, yet humane—and available to our common experience—too:

> The wayfarer,
> Perceiving the pathway to truth,
> Was struck with astonishment.
> It was thickly grown with weeds.
> "Ha," he said,
> "I see that none has passed here
> "In a long time."
> Later he saw that each weed
> Was a singular knife.
> "Well," he mumbled at last,
> "Doubtless there are other roads."

Of course Crane is not a major poet. He had neither a sustained poetic career nor any apparent desire for one. Sometimes his imagination paid out an unexpected poetic dividend while he lived for fiction. Nevertheless, as he was aware, these were his most personal, intimately revealing expressions. There are perhaps twenty of them to make up a body of perfectly genuine, wholly successful and individual, and extraordinarily intense poetry.

CHAPTER 6

The Red Badge of Courage

IN a way one could say that *The Red Badge of Courage,* Crane's masterpiece, was built of the romantic irony of the sketches, plus the complicit irony of *Maggie,* plus the imagistic fire of the poems, plus Crane's unexpectedly gifted historical imagination, plus his life-long intimations of war, plus a new heightening of his artistic powers and perceptions. But saying so, one would not have covered the ground—only have suggested some of the approaches to a work which has "made" all sorts of lists of "classics," sold fabulously (to whose enrichment?). It has engendered a body of criticism curiously inconsistent and stubborn, tending evermore (ignoring the merely eccentric) to repetition or, at best, to small variations on themes by somebody else. When was the last time anybody said anything both fresh and reasonably applicable about *The Red Badge of Courage?*

As other critics have demonstrated, much of this "criticism" will not meet the simplest tests of contextuality (one should be able to find warrant for what he "discovers" about the work in the fair context of the actual words of the text); coherence (the patterns discovered should make coherent sense in themselves, unless it is to be shown that the work is incoherent); and completeness (the interpretation should take cognizance of all the work and apply to all of it, not just some convenient fragment). The problem is by no means unique to Crane criticism, but for some critics self-validating intuition seems to replace a sense of responsibility to common, marketplace communication. One would think they were the artists. The resultant warfare has not been, however, without value; and some commentary has considerably cleared the atmosphere.

The problems to which Crane criticism has addressed itself are the traditional ones: Provenience—what are the sources of Crane's inspiration? Method—is the novel symbolistic, naturalistic, im-

117

pressionistic, realistic, or something else, and how successful is it as art? Meaning—what is the substance of the ideas presented or implied, and how does one prove his reading of them by solving the problems of structure, irony, and conclusion?

I

To match the literature which insists that Shakespeare must have been a lawyer to sketch Shallow, there has always been Road-to-Xanaduing about *The Red Badge of Courage*. The logic of the search is simple. Crane wrote impressively about war but hadn't seen any: he must have borrowed from other literature. As with *Maggie*, Continental "sources" have been popular despite Joseph Conrad's trenchant judgment: "I could not see the relevancy."[1] Almost any book about a lad who goes to war will do. Therefore, a number of American sources have been nominated.[2] Conrad's remark covers them, too. The real point seems to be that there lay a stratum of rather homogenized subliterary, semifictional Civil War memorials behind Crane's tale. He may have had some of them in mind when he first thought of his pot-boiler. But there is no reliable evidence that he had read any book about war other than *Battles and Leaders* before he wrote *The Red Badge*.

Much the same is true of guesses about where Crane got his title. Could it have been from Shakespeare's "Murder's crimson badge" in *Henry VI*—or is that a remote coincidence? Or was it from the red shoulder patch New Jersey's glamorous General Phil Kearney invented for his Third Corps?[3] Well, possibly, but in the Barrett manuscript, it is clear that Crane first called the novel "Private Fleming His Various Battles." He crossed that out and substituted the provocative, classic title apparently at the same time he went through the text cancelling the names of the soldiers wherever he could and abstracting them into "the tall soldier," "the loud soldier," "the youth," etc. In thinking back over his novel, Crane had had plenty of time to reflect upon his own phrase from Chapter Six, where deserter Fleming among the wounded "wished that he, too, had a wound, a little red badge of courage"—a "blighty" the Tommies called it in World War I because it sent them home a while with honor—and upon the pivotal irony of the unplanned fraudulence with which Fleming received the scalp wound, the necessary badge to let him back to his platoon with impunity.

No little of the source hunting, or of Crane "scholarship"

generally, suffers from an impression like that of Harvey Wickham's assurance that *George's Mother* was studied from Wickham's own very respectable relatives because "Frank" was seen by Crane to eat "George's amazing lunch—charlotte russe and a beer."[4] That would be dubious proof of the allegation at best. Unfortunately, it happens that "a Charlotte Russe and a glass of beer" was never George's lunch. It was the unpalatable offering of the equally unpalatable "Bowery jay" who tried to pick Maggie up after her first betrayal by Pete.[5]

Granting the sophistication necessary to have written what preceded *The Red Badge,* it is not clear that Crane had to have literary "sources." Obviously he had been fascinated by "Claverack's student batallion . . . the nucleus of that 'blue demonstration,' the very heart of his subsequent conception of an army."[6] His boyhood could scarcely have avoided middle-aged Grand Army of the Republic veterans, who were often as garrulous as they were ubiquitous in the 1880s. And Stephen would hardly have wished not to learn all he could of war from men who had been there. The most conspicuous of these was Crane's history teacher at Claverack, the "Reverend General" John B. Van Petten. He had advanced from chaplain to field officer in years of combat experience during the Civil War and been mustered out a brigadier. At Fair Oaks, Antietam, and Winchester he had seen not only hard fighting but many of the types of incidents used in *The Red Badge.* His after-dinner reminiscenses may have supplied the emotional, psychological coloring Crane indignantly missed from *Battles and Leaders.* In any case, Van Petten abundantly illustrates the oral tradition, the substance from the climate of his youth, which, with his personal concern for war, fear, and courage in life, would have been sufficient "source" for Crane had there been no other.[7]

II

It has been variously asserted that Crane's way of imagining and constructing *The Red Badge of Courage* was realist, naturalist, impressionist, or symbolist. It would make a difference if it could be demonstrated that one of them, or any other, was *the* method. One would then expect to interpret particular parts, and the whole, in certain ways, and one's reading and response would be affected accordingly. But the conviction with which these various views have been urged by sensitive and intelligent critics might in itself warn the reader that no unitary view is exclusively right. The very secret of the novel's power inheres in the inviolably organic uniqueness with which Crane adapted all four methods to his need. *The Red Badge's* method is all and none. There is no previous fiction like it.

The narrative point of view, however, is nothing new. James and Howells had been developing the technique used in *The Red Badge* for years; they repeatedly displayed it with an easy virtuosity which Crane could hardly have missed in the big magazines. In the earliest pages of *The Red Badge,* the storyteller's point of view, the narrative line-of-sight along events which will afford the reader's perspective, is permanently established. The voice is that of a third-person, "objective" narrator—not a first-person, "subjective" teller who says "Call me Ishmael" or "You don't know me without you have read a book. . ." But the point of view is located at almost the same place as if this were a first-person narrative: it is just behind the eyes of "the youthful private." The reader sees through Henry Fleming's eyes, and he is able to reflect backwards somewhat to record what goes on in Henry's mind (though never, of course, to overhear his "stream of consciousness"). But for the most part the reader is limited to seeing and hearing the life of the fiction as the narrator does; he can never "go behind" into the mind of another character.

These limitations make the experience afforded by the novel seem objective and thus credible, very intense, yet also somewhat detached and impersonal. The reader is not invited to "identify" wholly with young Fleming—a fact Joseph Hergesheimer recalled mourning over in his youth.[8] Fleming is part of a drama. He is to be subject to criticism, to judgment unintrusively unmoralized, established dramatically and ironically, but forcefully there. Essentially this is a perspective—but upon what? And to what end? What finally is the force of its proportion, its total form?

One way to begin to answer these questions is to notice some distinctions about the problem of point of view in this or any modern fiction which have not always been observed in discussing *The Red Badge*. At least four classes of "point of view" function in fiction. In simplest forms these are the author's, as he imagines and builds the work; the narrator's, which in any sophisticated fiction is not the author's way of looking at his work but an instrument of his technique in presenting it; the character's (or characters'), in the interplay of which—with one another and the narrator's viewpoints—lies a great deal of the craftsman's resource; and, finally, the reader's. Author's and reader's points of view are external to the novel. It may turn out that the reader's has been very skillfully played upon by the author who uses as instruments the internal points of view of narrator and characters.

The distinction in *The Red Badge of Courage* between the narrator's point of view and that of Henry Fleming, the sole character's view which the reader knows at all directly, is subtle for the reason already suggested. The narrator's point of view looks through Fleming's eyes. But though the reader sees what and as Fleming does, the reader is not he. Henry's point of view is that of his own experience; the reader knows it as, with the narrator, he goes reflexively "behind" for reports on that experience.

Material for observation of this experience is rich in the first four or five pages of the novel. It starts with a swiftly telescoped atmospheric registering of the context. Morning and early spring are telescoped in the first sentence:

The cold passed reluctantly from the earth, and the retiring fogs revealed an army stretched out on the hills, resting. As the landscape changed from brown to green, the army awakened, and began to tremble with eagerness at the noise of rumors. It cast its eyes upon the roads, which were growing from the long troughs of liquid mud to proper thoroughfares. A river, amber-tinted in the shadow of its banks, purled at the army's feet; and at night, when the stream had become of a sorrowful blackness, one could see across it the red, eye-like gleam of hostile camp-fires set in the low brows of distant hills.

It might, parenthetically, be possible to argue that the foregoing "one could see" establishes a narrative point of view distinct from Fleming's. But such an argument is unnecessarily messy and less than appreciative of Crane's artistic achievement. He handles point of view more like a movie camera than perhaps any predecessor had done. The reader stands to see somewhere back of Fleming's eyes. Sometimes the reader gets the long "panning" shot, sometimes the view only Henry could see, sometimes an interior view limited only by Crane's ignorance of methods Joyce would discover.

So the reader moves at once to a spirited, comic camp scene as tall Jim Conklin falsely reports imminent action. Then he retires with Fleming to ponder his emotions "in a little trance of astonishment" within the security of his hut. And suddenly his memory flashes back to the scenes and thoughts of his enlistment at home months before. The content of that flashback—seen by the reader through the narrator's double perception of what Fleming's point of view is now and what it was earlier—presents the basic problem of the novel.

The reader begins, then, with a perspective upon the perspectives of "the youth." They go back to dreams of battle and personal magnificence in war, dreams he has classed with "thought-images of heavy crowns and high castles"—the cloudy symbols of a high romance. Awake, this adolescent Minniver Cheevy "had long despaired of witnessing a Greek-like struggle. Such would be no more, he said. Men were better, or more timid. Secular and religious education had effaced the throat-grappling instinct, or else firm finance held in check the passions." On the farm, Fleming was a perfect neo-romantic.

Tales of "the war in his own country" inevitably began to move him, however. "They might not be distinctly Homeric, but there seemed to be much glory in them." In the face of his mother's Christian pacifism and her quietly effective ironic undercutting of his egotism, he eventually enlisted and left for camp with a soaring conviction "that he must be a hero." But the monotonous realities of camp life had taught him to concentrate on personal comfort and retreat "back to his old ideas. Greek-like struggles would be no more." Now, perhaps on the edge of the real thing, new possibilities of truth emerge. Maybe he will be a coward! "He felt that in this crisis his laws of life were useless. Whatever he had learned of himself was here of no avail. He was an unknown quantity. He saw that he would again be obliged to experiment as he had in early youth." When it turned out that the battle was not on the morrow, he had days to make "ceaseless calculations . . . all wondrously unsatisfactory." Examination of self and scrutiny of others were defeated. Only experience would help: "to go into the blaze, and then figuratively to watch his legs to discover their merits and faults . . . he must have blaze, blood, and danger, even as a chemist requires this, that and the other."

Except for the initial paragraph, the method and issues so far established are those of the realists. The emphasis on point of view, on vision, is theirs; and the establishment of a problem of knowledge, which will require an exercise in discovery and revelation, is theirs. So, too, is the pragmatic dependence on experience: answering the question by watching whether one's legs ran or stayed might have come straight from James's *Principles of Psychology*. And raising the issues of romanticism—the heroic, the glamorous, the egotistical, exalted and sentimental—was a confirmed habit of the realists. Anti-romanticism, the reduction by ridicule and irony of the romantic to the common, negative realism, was the first and always the easiest way for the realists to define themselves. Positive realism, finding the beauty, power, and meaning of life in the commonplace—a green farm boy among his peers in an unblooded regiment, for instance—was much more difficult. But the wrangling amateur military experts in the company street and the soldiers' hut are scenically presented—they talk and act—with a humorous precision dear to the heart of any lover of the common American man.

III

One does not read far into *The Red Badge of Courage*, however, without discovering that it is different from the traditional realistic novel. The extended and massive specification of detail with which the realist seems to impose upon one an illusion of the world of the common vision is wholly missing. Equally absent is the tremendous procession of natural and social "forces" characteristic of naturalism—of Frank Norris or Dreiser trying to be Zola. Detail is not absent, but it is comparatively sparingly deployed on a light, mobile structure; and it is used for intensive, not extensive effects. Reference to "forces" is there, but no effort at all to show them streaming in their mighty currents, floating the characters as tracers, as chips on the stream whose significance is to reveal the trending of the currents.

One of the more reliable ways, indeed, to distinguish romantic from realistic and both from naturalistic fiction is to examine the way each handles its characters. To the romancer the significance of his people is symbolic; they are representative men and women who reveal, by the doctrine of correspondence, spiritual truths (*viz.*, Chingachgook, Chillingworth, Goodman Brown, Captain Ahab and all his men). The reductive, agnostic realist, however, cannot believe in the spiritual sublimity, the ideality, of his characters. He levels his vision to the human, fascinated by the paradoxes of the common person: his individuality, his commonplace mediocrity, the representative, perhaps universal, meaning of his "common" moral problems. To the naturalist, finally, humanity means only animality. This is the ultimate reduction. Where the romancer's concern was superhuman and the realist's humane, the naturalist's is infrahuman. And in a sense the naturalist joins hands with the romancer (no matter how the latter might cringe) again in looking not so much to what the man is as to what he can be made to reveal about realities far larger, stronger, more important and more abstract than man.

In this intent, too, Crane stands with the realists, but he stands historically in advance of them toward the coming future of the novel. The critics of his own day who wondered if Crane did not represent a "new realism" may have been more than a little right.[9] It was natural, if not inevitable, that the realism of the generation previous to Crane should develop to prepare the way for its own displacement. The shift was toward an increasingly psychological realism, and it was propelled by at least two major forces. One of these was the displacement of positivism from its dominance of late nineteenth-century thought. A decade like the 1890's, which began with William James's *Psychology* and ended with the unleashing of the new, electronic factors in physics which produced Henry Adams' image of "himself lying in the Gallery of Machines at the Great Exposition of 1900, his historical neck broken by the sudden irruption of forces totally new," was bound at the least to loosen the grip of positivism on the imagination. The second force, however, arose from the practice of realistic fiction itself. The more one confronted the mystery of men as persons living out their fates and struggling toward their deaths, the more one's scrutiny turned from the outward sign to the inward process itself. Howells noticed in 1903, when he was writing a novel Freudian in all but specifically Viennese terminology for the main concept, that all the realists had of late been turning to psychology. Indeed, many of them had been flirting with psychic phenomena as far-flung as the claims of spiritualism. What he did not seem to notice was that he himself had been working largely in psychological realism since *The Shadow of a Dream* in 1891.

For the better part of thirty-five years, Howells had fought at the foremost point in a great battle to capture American taste for realism. He had defined realism as the objective truth in art about the visible aspects of human life. But in 1903 he registered his realization that a change had occurred among the great realists of the world. God seems to love the game of the pendulum in man's affairs, he observed. And now "A whole order of literature has arisen, calling itself psychological, as realism called itself scientific . . . it is not less evident in Tolstoi, in Gorky, in Ibsen, in Björnsen, in Hauptmann, and in Mr. Henry James, than in Maeterlinck himself."[10]

It was like Howells to leave himself out of the account. The surprising thing is his so registering the change almost fifteen years after he had launched himself into it. What he apparently did not see was that what he called "the present psychologism" was not just a providential swing of the pendulum but a fairly predictable outcome of the earlier realism—and that it was already bridging the way for the interior, stream of consciousness, and therefore symbolic fiction which would succeed it. The realism of which Howells had been the chief American prophet had been, as he said, "scientific" in the mid-nineteenth-century sense of factualistic and "objective." It had also been intensely humanistic, fixing its focus on persons, on characters, in their human dimensions, qualities, conflicts, problems, and fates. The more it fastened on characters and the visible evidence of inner conditions, the more that realism would be tempted to "go behind" as James said. The further behind the veil of sense it went, the less normally and normatively visible its evidences would be. After a while it would no longer be the realist's appeal to the common vision which would win the reader's suspension of disbelief, but only a faith in the realist's honesty of covert vision secured, perhaps, by his faithfulness to that common vision in overt matters. The turn to psychology opened important and exciting vistas to the accomplished realist like Henry James. It also paved the way for the displacement of realism by such masters to come as Joyce, Anderson, Lawrence, and Faulkner.

The Red Badge of Courage was the first masterpiece of that transition, as Howells imperfectly saw while reviewing it. Most commendable, he said, was "the skill shown in evolving from the youth's crude expectations and ambitions a quiet honesty and self-possession manlier and nobler than any heroism had imagined . . . and decidedly on the psychological side the book is worth while as an earnest of the greater things that we may hope for from a new talent working upon a high level, not quite clearly as yet, but strenuously."[11] In a lifetime devoted to part-time criticism, Howells had a high batting average, but this time he hit only a part of the ball. He may have been told or have divined Crane's interest in the psychological. Crane was able to be overt about it from Greece, telling John Bass that "Between two great armies battling against each other the interesting thing is the mental attitude of the men." Or, as he explained himself to his English readers, people "think they ought to demand" of "descriptions of battle" that they be placed "to stand in front of the mercury of war and see it rise or fall . . . but it is an absurd thing for a writer to do if he wishes to reflect, in any way, the mental condition of the men in the ranks. . . ."[12]

"To reflect . . . the mental condition of the men in the ranks," representing them especially with one youth, is an exact definition of the achievement—and probably the intention—of The Red Badge of Courage. Its formal structure is rather simply Aristotelian. It has a beginning (Chapters I-IV), which gets the youth to real battle; a middle (Chapters V-XIII), which witnesses his runaway and return; and an end (Chapters XIV-XXIII), which displays his achievement of "heroism" at climax, followed by a certain understanding of it in a coda-like final chapter. The middle and end sections are replete with notations of Fleming's psychological responses to fear, stress, and courage. There are progressively at least ninety such notations of Fleming's state of nerves-mind-psyche (it is not at all clear that Crane had any coherent psychological theory to exploit). They occur in pairs or triads of alternating or developmental stages as well as singly and are sometimes recurrent. If only by mere weight, the ninety constitute a major part of the substance of a short novel.

Actually, of course, psychological notations count for far more than mere bulk in The Red Badge. They are fascinating in themselves. For instance, Crane recorded something he no doubt picked up from football (as psychologists are said to have done later, naming the phenomenon "scrimmage blackout"). In the depth of combat, Crane supposed, Fleming would pass into an absorptive trance in which he was conscious of little but performed with intense automatism in a "battle-sleep" during which he might occasionally "dream" impressions. Essential to the achievement of the novel are the psychological patterns Crane divined for Fleming's combat experience. One is the obverse of the other. In the one, fear leads to panic, panic to guilt, guilt to rationalization and eventually to frustration and acquiescence. In the other, resentment produces rage, and rage "battle sleep"; resolution, including willingness to die, follows and leads in turn to "heroism" and at last to adumbrations of emotional realism and modesty. Equally striking are Crane's observations of the complexities of individual-group relations.

If this psychologism carried Crane past realism, it also defined his sense of naturalism, at least for this novel. Philosophic naturalism in

The Red Badge of Courage is not expounded. It is identifed as a form of romanticism, a buttress to the ego, a means of escape from moral reality and responsibility. In the end it is rejected. It is referred to—in the final state of the novel more obliquely than directly—so often as to leave little doubt that Crane was quite aware of its patterns of explanation and their potential uses. But it is at last only a foil for the pragmatic, relativistic ideas toward which the novel finally points.

It may also indicate Crane's decision about naturalism at this point to note that he cut most of the explicit references to its ideas out of *The Red Badge* at various stages of revision. Before Crane's manuscript, in the Barrett Collection at Virginia, was laminated in a doubtless necessary effort to save its crumbling paper, it was possible to work out theoretically the existence of at least seven progressive states of *The Red Badge* text. Without being able to know what preceded the text which Crane's poverty preserved in canceled fragments on the versos of a later start, we have (on legal foolscap) the earliest draft. It existed in four states, having been revised in pen, in pencil, and at last in blue crayon. Unfortunately, I am informed, the essential color variations were lost in the lamination process: how very much too bad that no one thought to preserve the colors as they have been saved in the far more complex facsimile of *Walt Whitman's Blue Book!*[13]

Somewhere in the progression some leaves came out for the Bacheller syndicated text. And before the first edition there was a now lost typescript with nobody knows how much revision. At last, of course, Crane read and must in some degree have revised the galley proofs, which have also disappeared.

Rather boldly explicit in draft but variously suppressed and left implicit in the final text was Crane's association of philosophic naturalism with Henry Fleming's panic syndrome. One may guess that he thought to make the resultant theme central to the novel's development and then changed his mind.

Early in the morning of his first battle day, Fleming dashes, wild with curiosity, upon the scene of what he expects will be immediate combat. But it is bathos, nothing really is happening; and as the regiment presses on into a silently ominous landscape, his courage oozes away: "This advance upon Nature was too calm . . . absurd ideas took hold upon him. . . . It was all a trap." With this comes the idea associated throughout: he must become a prophet of the truth "Nature" reveals. "He thought that he must break from the

ranks and harangue his comrades. . . . The generals were
idiots. . . . There was but one pair of eyes in the corps." But fear
of ridicule silences him as the tense ranks advance "to look at war,
the red animal—war, the blood-swollen god." However, nature is
no constant for Fleming; she varies with his psychic states. After his
first and successful combat, he wakes from his battle-sleep with "a
flash of astonishment at the blue pure sky and the sun gleaming on
the trees and fields. It was surprising that Nature had gone tranquil-
ly on with her golden process in the midst of so much devilment."

Fleming's later efforts to appeal to nature as a constant and as a
source of comforting revelation (or rationalization) are therefore
doomed. If one were to argue from *The Red Badge of Courage*
about Crane's attitudes toward the naturalistic argument for man's
animal irresponsibility toward duty and morality he would, in fact,
have to conclude that Crane had considered but repudiated that
argument.

Chapter VII is the first decisively interesting surviving example of
Crane's revision of *The Red Badge*, and the revisions affect precisely this issue, shifting from explicit to implicit. This is the chapter in
which Fleming is plunged from unworthy hope of personal justifica-
tion into shame and self-pity by his deserted comrades' holding
their line and repulsing the attack from which he had run. He seeks
to "bury himself" in the thick woods, in nature. There he passes
through swift changes of mood. "This landscape gave him assurance. A fair field holding life. It was the religion of peace.
. . . He conceived Nature to be a woman with a deep aversion to
tragedy." He shies a pine-cone at "a jovial squirrel" who dashes for
safety: "The youth felt triumphant at this exhibition. There was the
law, he said. Nature had given him a sign. . . . Nature was of his
mind."

As he wanders on, however, other signs obtrude. In a swamp he
sees "a small animal pounce in and emerge directly with a gleaming
fish." And finally, in what at first seems "a chapel" in a pine grove,
he finds the disintegrating corpse of a Federal soldier from a bygone
battle, with "black ants swarming greedily upon the grey face."
The present text ends abruptly with Fleming fleeing the horror and
leaving "the chapel" to the "soft wind" and "sad silence" of
nature—which ties in perfectly with an impressionistic bit of atmosphere about the onset of twilight which begins the next chapter.

Once, however, the text had been far more intellectually obvious,
and Crane had kept it that way for quite a while. The manuscript,

at least in its third state, was revised first in pen, then in pencil. In that minimally fifth revision Crane cancelled from the end of the chapter these words,

> Again the youth was in despair. Nature no longer condoled with him. There was nothing, then, after all, in that demonstration she gave—the frightened squirrel fleeting aloft from the missile. He thought . . . that there was given another law which far-overtopped it—all life existing upon death, eating ravenously, stuffing itself with the hopes of the dead. . . .[14]

That mood also passed. Shortly he is thinking as he heads back toward the battle that, because brambles restrain him, "Nature could not be quite ready to kill him." But, of course, that alternation was lost from the revised text.

Fleming's nightmare agony in the middle part of *The Red Badge* climaxes in Chapter IX with the macabre death of Conklin, "the tall soldier," and in Chapter X with Fleming's desertion of "the tattered man" on being asked where his own wound was. Crane tried hard to provide Fleming with reflections adequate to his shocked and shame-sodden state but he failed, cancelling, rewriting, and cancelling again. He had Henry reflect, in utter opposition to his old romantic ideas, that soldiers were really "Nature's dupes." Nature went seducing men with "dreams" of "glory," defeating their ingenuity of devices to stave off death by planting a treacherous sentiment in their hearts. "War, he said bitterly to the sky, was a makeshift created because ordinary processes could not furnish deaths enough." From earlier hints, Crane seems to have developed this and Fleming's derisive fury about it for five pages.[15] He cancelled the effort out only in the blue-crayon revision which appears to have gone to the typist.

That cancelled experience of Fleming's lay behind the returned motif of his exaltation of self-justification at seeing, at the beginning of Chapter XI, the routed troops on the road. That feeling is followed at once by his feeling like a sinner in Hell watching angels "with weapons of flame and banners of sunlight" when a disciplined column of infantry butts its glorious way through the chaos. Crane stops to put Fleming through nine progressive states of psychosomatic and imaginary response to his situation in the least dramatic (and so perhaps least satisfactory) chapter in the book. And it was clearly Crane's early intention to follow the "analytic" chapter with a twelfth which would bring to an ironic climax both the theme of natural irresponsibility and the several times repeated theme of Fleming's prophetic role toward his comrades and the world. Since the relative slackness of the previous chapter makes it clear that discursive patches mar *The Red Badge,* it is not surprising that Crane suppressed his intended Chapter XII. He was right to do so, and the principal use of considering it is to see that in it he unmistakably derided the naturalistic diagnosis of Fleming's condition together with Henry's Dreiser-like urge to proclaim its gospel. And he left (now submerged) that rejection as the pivot upon which Fleming could turn again, now fit to be delivered by kindly (but by no means unique, as it turned out) fates to his outfit.

That aborted chapter begins, "It was always clear to Fleming that he was entirely different from other men," and now he consoles himself that his suffering has been "unprecedented" in the awful opposition of his tiny self to the universe. But then he sees that there is no malice really, "merely law," and that there were compensating principles—what might be called the squirrel's law recurred to him:

Nature had provided her creations with various defenses and ways to escape . . . that the things might resist or hide with a security proportionate to their strength and wisdom. It was all the same old philosophy. He could not omit a small grunt of satisfaction as he saw with what brilliancy he had reasoned it all out.

Soon he is ready to avail himself of that brilliancy and apply his findings to the incident of his own flight from the battle: "It was not a fault; it was a law. It was—But he saw that when he had made a vindicating structure of great principles, it was the calm toes of tradition that kicked it all down about his ears." In bitter rebellion he then resolves to save mankind from the worship of "the gods of the ashes," and he begins to see himself "the growing prophet of a world-reconstruction. Far down in the pure depths of his being . . . he saw born a voice. He conceived a new world, modelled by the pain of his life, in which no old shadows fell darkening upon the temple of thought. And there were many personal advantages in it."

He thinks of "piercing orations" and "himself a sun-lit figure upon a peak." But gradually his enthusiasm burns out as he thinks of mankind's bovine habitude—"he would be beating his fists against the brass of accepted things." He rails abuse "in supreme disgust and rage. . . . To him there was something terrible and

awesome in these words spoken from his heart to his heart. He was
very tragic."[16]

Crane's irony is obvious from the bathetic anti-climaxes of this:
"And there were many personal advantages . . . a sun-lit figure.
. . . He was very tragic." But even though this has disappeared
from the text, its irony remains operative in the pivotal next
chapter. There Fleming suddenly sees that all-enviable, heroic-
angelic column charging back from the fray "like terrified buf-
faloes." He feels "horror-stricken" and stares "in agony and
amazement." Then, most significantly, "He forgot that he was
engaged in combating the universe. He threw aside his mental
pamphlets on the philosophy of the retreated and rules for the
guidance of the damned." He loses himself in concern for the
stricken angels, thinks absurdly of rallying them, tries to detain one
to ask what happened, and gets his red badge of courage from the
rifle-butt in the hands of a hysterical ex-hero. His knockout is virtually a death, and for a while after he goes "tall soldier fashion."
His first day of combat draws on to sunset, and in the dark he is
rescued by the selfless and faceless "cheery soldier" and delivered
back to the 304th New York where he belongs.

There he is met with new cheer and sympathy. His lie about being shot readily believed, he is nursed and cared for by a suddenly
mature, modest and no longer loud Wilson. In the morning he discovers that perhaps half the regiment had been missing after the action but turned up by morning with stories—" 'Jest like you
done,' " Wilson tells Fleming. Then, in a very late, blue-crayon
cancellation he thinks "with deep contempt of all his grapplings
and tuggings with fate and the universe." He sees how ridiculous
had been the cherished uniqueness and novelty of his thought. But
he begins to feel self-respect returning, since he is safe and
"unimpeached."[17]

It will take all the rest of the last part of the book to try that
egotism in the fire of a real, if minor, heroism and reduce it to the
human modesty achieved by Wilson on the first day. From this
point forward, however, nature will be no more abstracted, per-
sonified, or capitalized in *The Red Badge*, and Fleming's recollections of his prophetic ideas and role will be merely embarrassed. He
will be glad nobody else knows. Intellectually, that seems to be
what there is to naturalism in the novel, and the symbolic or impressionistic uses of it are keyed to the intellectual.

It seems clear that *The Red Badge* is not a work of naturalism;

and it is also certain that Fleming is *not* "guided by a naturalistic
code of ethics." No more is a naturalistic "Henry's attitude . . .
characteristic of Crane."[18] The true naturalist's truth must be that
man is a part of nature and not other. Crane's sense of the indifference or hostility of nature to man was shared, for instance, by
a Pilgrim Father (Brewster), a Massachusetts Bay Puritan
(Winthrop), a rationalistic Calvinist (Edwards), a deist (Freneau,
"The Hurricane"), by Melville (whatever he was), and by many
varieties of non-naturalistic Darwinists. Like them, Crane did
believe man was "other"—in Crane's case, man was human. That
was a lesson Henry Fleming learned to see.

IV

Then it becomes possible to say that *The Red Badge of Courage*
is a unique work of psychological realism deeply affected in style by
the fact that the author was an ironic, imagistic, metaphysical poet.
And that brings one to the moot questions of Crane's impressionism
and symbolism. If one could be sure of the qualities of these, it
would be best to treat them apart. Since, in fact, their existence as
well as their separability is obscure, it may be best to take them
together. Actually, in Crane's case it might be impossible to define
his impressionism and symbolism separately.

"Impressionism" was a potent and intensely controversial term in
the 1890s. A war cry for those who sought escape from Victorianism,
it stood for the liberation of the artist from the academy and tradition, from formalism and ideality, from narrative, and finally even
from realism; for realism demanded responsibility to the common
vision and impressionism responsibility only to what the unique eye
of the painter saw. It was also a swearword for conservatives of
every variety, of course. In painting there was a solid body of
reference, forged in the heat of often vicious controversy, and a
body of distinguished (no matter how controversial) examples to
give substance to "impressionism."

But in literature the case was and is different. There was a rather
vague breeze of the *avant garde* ghosting in the American literary
atmosphere of the 1890s. In 1890 itself the Harpers published a
volume of *Pastels in Prose from the French*, translated by Stuart
Merrill with an introduction by Howells. It presented pieces by
Baudelaire, Daudet, and Mallarmé, with a number of *chinoiseries*

by Judith Gautier. The collection set Howells to musing about the Prose Poem, poetic prose, and poetry in prose and concluding that "the very life of the form is its aerial delicacy, its soul is that perfume of thought, of emotion, which these masters here have never suffered to become an argument."

Even if one assumed for the sake of the argument that Crane read the volume, what could it be said that he learned from it? The question resembles the unstudied one of whether, even as poet, Crane learned anything from the strikingly new poems Howells was publishing between 1891 and 1895 under such *avant-gardiste* rubrics as "Moods," "Monochromes," "Pebbles," and, in three cases, "Impression." On January 16, 1897, the *Chicago Record*, for example, damned *The Little Regiment* because it showed that "Mr. Crane is not a scientist. . . . He is above all an impressionist." But safely in England with Joseph Conrad and Edward Garnett, Crane could if he wished take pleasure in the fact that with them the epithet was a high compliment.[19]

Nevertheless, it was and is difficult to know just what Crane's "impressionism" means. In literature the term is so vague and so devoid of explicit example as not even to make an entry in Wellek and Warren, *Theory of Literature*, or in standard histories. Handbook definitions, when they occur, are not conspicuous for relevance to Crane. They seem roughly agreed that in literature "impressionism" means either absence of detail or else the effect of the author observing himself in the presence of life, not the life. Neither applies illuminatingly to the work of Stephen Crane. Yet it would be strange if there were nothing meant by all the often impressive critics who have applied the term to Crane; and of course that is not the case.

What they are talking about comes down, perhaps, to the vividness and intensity of Crane's notation of atmospheric textures and to the striking economy, *multum in parvo*, of his form. No doubt the effort to achieve psychological realism promoted what Willa Cather brilliantly defined as "The Novel Démeublé."[20] Howells's first attempts at it in *The Shadow of a Dream* (1890) and *An Imperative Duty* (1892) were strikingly "disfurnished" after *A Hazard of New Fortunes* (1890). Crane's own comment on literary aims is characteristically minimal and apparently innocent of the term "impressionism" until his significant work had been done—and Conrad, Garnett, Heuffer, and others had explained the situation to him. Even then he confined a striking use of it to painterly reference:

The church had been turned into a hospital for Spanish wounded who had fallen into American hands. The interior of the church was too cave-like in its gloom for the eyes of the operating surgeons, so they had had the altar-table carried to the doorway, where there was a bright light. Framed then in the black archway was the altar-table with the figure of a man upon it. He was naked save for a breech-clout, and so close, so clear was the ecclesiastic suggestion that one's mind leaped to a fantasy that this thin, pale figure had just been torn down from a cross. The flash of the impression was like light, and for this instant it illumined all the dark recesses of one's remotest idea of sacrilege, ghastly and wanton. I bring this to you merely as an effect, an effect of mental light and shade, if you like; something done in thought similar to that which the French impressionists do in color; something meaningless and at the same time overwhelming, crushing, monstrous.[21]

It has been persuasively argued that Crane must have learned much and adapted to his writing what he learned of French Impressionism.[22] Yet Linson, who should certainly have known, denies it flatly—and apparently by implication denies the name of "painter" to Vosburgh and the "Indians." Linson had been a fellow student of Gauguin but not wholly in sympathy with him. At least, however, Linson must be supposed to have known what Impressionism was about:

To the oft repeated query as to Crane's use of color: "Did he get it from his studio associates?" My answer is "No." I was the only painter among his early intimates; one or two others he met casually with me. The rest were illustrators or journalists. . . . The Impressionism of that day was to him an affectation, and all affectation was dishonesty, uncreative, and thus dead from the start.[23]

That statement might, of course, be regarded at most as authoritative only through Crane's establishment of himself in England.

Taken at fullest value, however, Linson indicates the same things shown by Crane's remark about Oscar Wilde: Wilde was "a mildewed chump." Crane was having none of the official *fin de siècle*. But he might equally well have had nonetheless his own sort of impressionism; and one can catch him at it. In "War Memories," again, there is a peculiar little moment when one almost feels embarrassed for Crane:

"But to get the real thing!" cried Vernall, the war correspondent. "It seems impossible! It is because war is neither magnificent nor squalid; it is simply life, and an expression of life can always evade us. We can never tell life, one to another, although sometimes we think we can." [24]

Those Shelleyan cries and the self-consciousness about expression and the real thing are out of character for Crane. And, as a matter of fact, they constitute a strategic insincerity. He is embarking on a long series of pictures which will not "tell life" but present it unmistakably to a reader.

Actually Crane had, quite consciously, mastered the solution to that (as presented) pseudoproblem long before. In the *New York World* for October 15, 1896, for instance, he had lightened a bit of journalism for himself with a touch of virtuosity:

We, as a new people, are likely to conclude that our mechanical perfection, our structural precision, is certain to destroy all quality of sentiment in our devices, and so we prefer to grope in the past when people are not supposed to have had any structural precision. As the terrible, the beautiful, the ghastly, pass continually before our eyes we merely remark that they do not seem to be correct in romantic detail.

But an odor of oiled woods, a keeper's tranquil, unemotional voice, a broom stood in the corner near the door, a blue sky and a bit of moving green tree at a window so small that it might have been made by a canister shot—all these ordinary things contribute with subtle meaning to the horror of this comfortable chair, this commonplace bit of furniture that . . . waits and waits.

The subject is the electric chair at Sing Sing, and the virtuosity is that he has solved the expressive problem in the act of describing it.

Not to choose any of the nature descriptions which set the atmospheric stage so perfectly over and again in *The Red Badge* or which tally Fleming's psychic gyrations, one bit of Crane's special impressionism, his way of conveying the real thing with extraordinary intensity, may stand for dozens. The 304th New York has not quite gone into action when nearby "Saunders" gets "crushed" by Confederates:

The flag suddenly sank down as if dying. Its motion as it fell was a gesture of despair.

Wild yells came from behind the walls of smoke. A sketch in gray and red dissolved into a mob-like body of men who galloped like wild horses.

With minimal but exact detail, in an aura of psychological, not objective, reality, the experience is precisely, forcefully communicated. The method is more poetic than traditionally novelistic, as has been variously observed. It is Crane's impressionism of texture. For the rest, the question has been most usefully approached through William M. Gibson's citation of the letter from Thomas Wolfe to Scott Fitzgerald dividing great writers into "putter-inners" and "taker-outers."[25] Crane belongs with Flaubert, Hemingway, and Willa Cather's ideal as a "taker-outer," and that trait perhaps is the other aspect of his impressionism.

Inescapably, when one considers Crane's abruptly vivid effects, the question arises whether they are just impressionistically textural or symbolic as well. In some senses, of course, they are immitigably symbolic, just as any word, any significant cluster of words, is symbolic in any literary context. But surely that is not what is meant when Crane is called a "symbolist," for it would distinguish him not at all from any other author. In fact, to make the point one last time, it is hard to say what species, if any, of "symbolist" Crane was. No systematic discussion of that subject appears to exist. Certainly, as visionist, he represented the opposite of Charles Feidelson's "symbolistic imagination" and so he represents the opposite of Mallarmé, Baudelaire, et seq.[26] Crane was, that is, intensely concerned with the vision of realities, objective and subjective, which he regarded as independent of language but ideally susceptible of "unmistakable" communication through words. The evidence seems clear that he had no notion of any linguistically self-contained and unique literary "reality" and that he would have found that notion laughably conceited. One might, of course, argue, as exponents of some antirational schools of criticism appear to do, that, regardless of what Crane thought he thought, he was a "symbolist" because all good literature is such and so successful authors are this (or that) because their literature is good. But arguments of that sort are not available to discussion.

Thoroughly discussable, however, is what has become virtually a school of Crane criticism which follows the original ideas of the single most energetic and embattled of Crane scholar-critics, Robert W. Stallman. One can scarcely avoid concentrating discussion of the master, his disciples, and their doctrine on the problem of the most famous image in *The Red Badge of Courage*, now almost the best known image in American literature: "The red sun was pasted in the sky like a wafer."

Stallman's intuition that this is the central characterizing symbol of the whole work, from which the nature and stature of its artistry and the substance of its meaning must be interpreted, was promulgated in a forty-nine page introduction in the *Omnibus* (175 - 224). For Stallman the key to it all is that the "wafer" means the form of bread, circular, crisp, almost parchmentlike, used in the celebration of the Eucharist in liturgical churches: "I do not think it can be doubted that Crane intended to suggest here the sacrificial death celebrated in communion." From this he argued back that Jim Conklin, the tall soldier who has died in the passages just preceding Crane's introduction of the image, is Christ, or a Christ-figure, and that the book then becomes, as Daniel Hoffman, accepting Stallman, said, "a chronicle of redemption." The contention is that, as in Christian doctrine, Fleming is somehow redeemed by the sacrificial death of Conklin in a symbolic or "apocalyptic" novel richly laden with Christian reference.

It should cause no wonder that such views have been not only doubted but challenged. A small critical war has been waged over them, with the balance appearing to turn firmly against them. The symbolist critics have obviously been useful in correcting overemphases on Crane's "naturalism," in stimulating study of his artistry, and in calling attention to achievements in that art which rise beyond what is usually subsumed under "impressionism." One thinks twice before rejecting the discoveries of well-informed, critically sensitive commentators. And it would be arrogant to deny that the childhood training and imaginative affinities of Stephen Crane should have led him to Christian imagery, or even perhaps to a pattern of Christian symbolism in *The Red Badge*. But, in all candor, many other critics simply cannot find such interpretations valid. The evidence adduced for the symbolic pattern breaks down at every point and at the first scrutiny. It is in fact not clear, first of all, that Crane as Crane is ever truly a symbolist: the test case may be "The Open Boat." Perhaps one needs to extend the sense of "impressionism" to take in what Crane does with images.

It would require a separate book to argue the problem out, but one can sketch the approaches to the problem by sticking to the wafer and Jim Conklin. To begin with, it was inherently improbable that Crane thought of a "wafer" as eucharistic. He had been reared

in an antiliturgical, enthusiastically anti-Catholic church and had
become hotly anticlerical. While one could not rule out his knowing
of the wafer of the Mass, he was much more likely to have thought
of the word as denoting a confection or, as various critics have
pointed out, an item of stationery common to and typical of the
nineteenth century. As messy, expensive sealing wax passed out of
use, it was replaced by a useful imitation of paper or other substance. Round, with neatly serrated edges stylizing the irregularities
of a wax seal, often a deep, solid red as wax had been, these often
gummed "wafers" were used to seal letters, packages, documents,
diplomas, etc. See definition 3 as opposed to definition 4 in the
Merriam-Webster unabridged *Dictionary of the English Language,*
Second Edition, for an unmistakable distinction between the
stationer's (and Crane's) usage (no. 3) and the liturgical (and
Stallman's) usage (no. 4). Joseph Hergesheimer, reading Crane,
"thought of an actual red wafer, such as druggists fixed to their
bottles; it had a definite, a limited size for me, an established, clear
vermilion color."[27]

Visualizing *that* kind of "wafer" expunges religious siginificance
from the image, and it removes certain embarrassments, too. If the
image were to be taken as seriously sacramental, why was it red?
And if one strained toward a metaphysical answer to that, why then,
was it surrealistically "pasted"? Not to mention the most painful
lapse in mere taste, there are embarrassments in the argument that
the Lincolnesque Conklin is meant to represent Christ. As with the
wafer, the connections seem hopelessly imprecise. Conklin does not
bear the stigmata of Christ—even in his side. Christ's side was
pierced after death by the spear of a professional soldier,
iconography shows a neat, clean incision. Conklin's "side looked as
if it had been chewed by wolves." Nor will it do to argue that the
sign is Fleming's recognition scream, "Gawd! Jim Conklin!" Thirteen lines later, Conklin is saying, ". . . Lord, what a circus! An' b'
jiminey, I got shot. . . . " Soldiers in *The Red Badge*, like real
soldiers, frequently take the name of the Lord their God in
vain—speaking not with symbolic portentousness any more than
with blasphemous intent but simply as they speak (not in *The Red
Badge*) obscenities for the registration of stereotyped and often
comically inappropriate emotions.

The decisive difficulties with the Christian-symbolist reading of
The Red Badge, it seems, are that there appears to be no way to
make a coherent account of the symbols as referential to Christian

doctrine and then to match that with what happens in the novel. The Christian doctrines of redemption and atonement, however central to orthodox faith, have ever been theologically obscure, intellectually mysterious. But they have always also been vital to Christian experience. And there just isn't any evidence of that, particularly as associated with the wafer and Conklin's death, in the after development of *The Red Badge*. There is textually no evidence that Fleming so much as perceives the "wafer." He mentions Conklin only once, informing Wilson of Jim's death, and they mourn briefly in the fashion of combat soldiers in the midst of death, ". . . poor cuss!" Restored to self-esteem on his safe return to the regiment, Fleming quickly soars into an arrogance unpleasantly contrasted with Wilson's quiet manliness. At the end he has self-admiration to place beside humiliation as objects of contemplation. But it is his desertion of the live but dying tattered man which stabs his conscience. Conklin's death is absent from his thoughts.

It may be, in short, that Crane had no notion conscious or unconscious of "redemption" for Fleming. That may not have been his point at all, and the fact that one can gather a great deal of religious reference—or any other sort of reference—from the text may imply no hidden cohesions of meaning. Or it may: perhaps it is more a matter of whether one cares for Miss Caroline Spurgeon's methods with Shakespeare or not.

But in the end, the trouble with a "symbolic" reading of *The Red Badge* is that it assumes some sort of operative attitude toward a referential reality on the part of the artist. No matter how one qualifies it, a literary symbol must somehow be an image which points to something else, something usually conceptual. That "other" may be an established mythology accepted by artist and public; but nobody supposes that sort of integrative symbolism possible to Crane with Christianity. Or the artist may be in revolt, and the symbols disintegrative of the mythology—as dominantly in Melville. Or the symbols may refer to an arcane, even unique, mythology of the artist—in which case the interpreter must either be blanked or find the key to the arcanum.

The arcane way of a Blake or Yeats seems foreign to the temperament and known ideals of Crane. But it may be that symbolistic investigation of that possibility and of the disintegrative functions of Crane's religious imagery might prove more fruitful than those which have hitherto apparently assumed integrative patterns.

Howells may well have been deeply perceptive in remarking that Crane had not yet got into the secret of himself. It might be possible to divine part of that secret by guessing at where Crane's religious insights were, perhaps unconsciously, leading him. On the other hand, humanistic and naturalistic interpreters have no doubt been right in seeing how the vision of *The Red Badge* scouted and reduced traditional religious as well as romantic securities. Perhaps such should pay more attention to the imagery as symbol.

In any case, symbolic or not, Crane's imagery has obviously only begun to be comprehended. With a bewildering richness of reference (infraconceptual and so at first level imagistic and not symbolic), he wove a dense texture in *The Red Badge of Courage*. That, and not the often startling locutions, constitutes the triumph of its style. *The Red Badge* focuses only on three soldiers, Fleming and two who are obviously foils for him. One of them, Wilson, goes swiftly through the evolution from "loud soldier" to clear-sighted and therefore modest manhood which "The Veteran" testifies that Fleming also attained, perhaps by the end of the novel. But Wilson's transformation occurs while our eyes, which are with Fleming, are absent. Partly they are occupied with the death of "the spectral soldier," Jim Conklin.

If these common soldiers are representative as well as ordinary persons, Conklin is the representative sacrificed soldier, and he occupies in the novel a place equivalent to that of the Unknown Soldier in the national pantheon. His death deserves the emphasis its drama provides in *The Red Badge*. It is, as it must be, an occasion for shock and protest. Fleming incoherently registers it: "The youth turned, with sudden, livid rage, toward the battle field. He shook his fist. He seemed about to deliver a philippic. 'Hell—' " And nature, as it generally does in the novel, registers Fleming—the awful intensity but faceless frustration of the shock which cannot yet be grief: "The red sun was pasted in the sky like a wafer."

V

If style be taken as texture and form as structure, the question of the equal success of the novel's form depends on deciding the much-discussed problem of the ending. Does the novel end well? Does it end or just disappear? Is there a climax? Is the ending of the novel satisfactory, in short, in emphasis and substance?

Debate has raged since the early reviews, and much of it around the last chapter. Though many critics have not troubled to mention it, few would deny the real achievement of a climax in personal victory which comes at the end of the next to the last chapter. Jeered at by veterans, scorned by their general as "mud-diggers" and "mule drivers," barely surviving after a temporary desertion rate of nearly fifty percent on the first day, close to a "pretty success" which they had funked by a hundred feet a little earlier, the regiment had stood exasperatedly under a last pressure. Fleming, now a color-bearer, had resolved "that his final and absolute revenge was to be a- chieved by his dead body lying, torn and gutttering, upon the field." His lieutenant had continued to curse, but it was now "with the air of a man who was using his last box of oaths."

Then the men are ordered to charge and at last, tough, deter- mined, sacrificial, soldier-like, they really do. Fleming forces the way, banner in hand, and Wilson captures the colors of the enemy. There arose "wild clamorings of cheers. The men gesticulated and bellowed in ecstasy." They had even taken prisoners. Fleming and Wilson sat "side by side and congratulated each other." The narrative progression has been simple. Beginning in doubt about Fleming's—and the regiment's—courage, it had sunk to despair with his cowardice and Conklin's death. Now it rises to climax in their clear success, even, in a minimal sense, their heroism. The reversed curve is classic. And even more so is the reflective short downward curve of anticlimax at the end as the regiment is recalled and starts to wind its way back over the river and the men can suddenly realize that the battle is over.

As Fleming realizes this, his mind clears of "battle-sleep," and he is able to take stock. Crane trimmed quite a lot from the manuscript of the last chapter, much of it reflecting too exactly the naturalistic debates he also cut. But only one of the cuts was really important. What he was doing with Fleming, it seems clear, was not holding him up for judgment but rounding off the account of his ex- perience. It was out of the question for Crane, insofar as he was a realist, to end a plot. It was neither with abstract structure nor with fable that he was concerned. The realists saw life as a continuum of the personal experiences of their characters. One broke in upon its flow at one significant point and left it at another. If in the course of this, one had any ulterior ideological motives, they should be planted out of sight and left for the reader to find.

As realist—psychological realist—as impressionist, perhaps even as metaphysician, Crane was, as we have seen, a visionist. The important thing was to see pellucidly and honestly. And what Crane is concerned with at the end of *The Red Badge* is what Fleming can see. By letting the readers see what Fleming sees, Crane will let them decide what to think of him. Henry struggles "to marshal all his acts. . . . From this present point of view he was enabled to look upon them with some correctness, for his new condition had already defeated certain sympathies."

Supposing that the defeated sympathies are the multitude of earlier romanticisms, what does Fleming's cleared sight now reveal in those three ultimate pages of the novel? That his "public deeds" were glorious and impart a "thrill of joy" to his ego. But that he has incurred real shame, however hidden, for "his flight" and real guilt for the tattered soldier, "he, who blind with weariness and pain, had been deserted in the field." This vision and the fear of some impossible detection balance his self-glorification with "a wretched chill of sweat" and "a cry of sharp irritation and agony."

In the end he sees that he is neither a hero nor a villain, that he must assume the burdens of a mixed, embattled, impermanent, modest, yet prevailing humanity. He has discovered courage:

> . . . gradually he mustered force to put the sin at a distance. And at last his eyes seemed to open to some new ways. He found that he could look back upon the brass and bombast of his earlier gospels and see them truly. He was gleeful when he discovered that he now despised them.
>
> With this conviction came a store of assurance. He felt a quiet manhood, non-assertive but of sturdy and strong blood. He knew that he would no more quail before his guides, wherever they should point. He had been to touch the great death, and found that, after all, it was but the great death. He was a man.

If capturing the enemy flag climaxes the action of *The Red Badge*, this discovery of manliness concludes its exploration of ideas. The third major theme could not be concluded, however, since Fleming was not dead. It was the continuing notation of Fleming's psychological states which could only be harmonized in a sort of fade-out chord as Milton had done with the last lines of "Lycidas." Trying to force more out of these last sentences than Crane put there has caused unnecessary trouble for critics.

As he trudged away from "blood and wrath" Fleming's "soul changed"—as it had changed sometimes three times in a page earlier in the novel, though with more prospect of duration (not per-

manence) this time. Crane tried to end this three times before he
got it right. Finally he showed Fleming turning to a vision—"with a
lover's thirst to images of tranquil skies, fresh meadows, cool
brooks—an existence of soft and eternal peace." And a nature-
image ends the book as one had begun it, the endlessly shifting
nature registering the never settled psychological state in the last
words. "Over the river a golden ray of sun came through the hosts
of leaden rain clouds."

Was Henry Fleming then a hero? Well, yes—and no. It wasn't
quite Crane's business to say so in *The Red Badge*, and he let it go
to "The Veteran," which Eric Solomon very properly calls "A Gloss
on *The Red Badge of Courage*."[28] There the reader sees that
modesty, candor about his "flight," and a quiet courage to do what
a man must do mark the veteran with the perspective of more
battles and many years—as in two days they could never plausibly
have marked "the youth." The ambiguities of Fleming's situation
are natural. But Crane's irony bites only at his past delusions. He
has become entitled to "images" of flowery peace.

The essence of that irony is that it would have been impossible
for the early Fleming to judge whether the boy who had both "run"
and borne the colors was hero or poltroon. He wouldn't, in fact,
have known what he was talking about. He wouldn't have been
able to see. From another point of view, Henry's heroism at its last
is only common, the ordinary stock of courage among fighting men
(or among truly living men and women), where what the visionless
think "heroism" is as common as breathing. But from yet another
point of view, the courage it takes to be human in the face of all the
odds *is* magnificent, as only the extraordinarily sharp and realizing
vision perceives. And it was Crane's sense of that in *The Red Badge*,
as in much of the best of his work, which gives it an elevation and a
pungency often tragic and always memorable. He talked about it
overtly in "War Memories":

On the morning of July 2, I sat on San Juan Hill and watched Laughton's
division come up. . . . There wasn't a high heroic face among them. They
were all men intent on business. That was all. It may seem to you that I am
trying to make everything a squalor. That would be wrong. I feel that
things were often sublime. But they were *differently* sublime. They were
not of our shallow and preposterous fictions. They stood out in a simple,
majestic commonplace. It was the behavior of men on the street. It was the
behavior of men. In one way, each man was just pegging along at the heels
of the man before him, who was pegging along at the heels of still another

man, who was pegging along at the heels of still another man who—It was that in the flat and obvious way. In another way it was pageantry, the pageantry of the accomplishment of naked duty. One cannot speak of it—the spectacle of the common man serenely doing his work, his appointed work. It is the one thing in the universe which makes one fling expression to the winds and be satisfied to simply feel.

This passage was written at the end, when Crane was sick unto death and worn down to talking about it. In *The Red Badge of Courage* he was at a peak of his creative powers and could simply master the imaginations of readers with the power of an astonishing young genius presenting a masterpiece.

After The Red Badge of Courage

THAT sense of the ambiguous sublimity of courageous life in the face of the common fate, and the *Maggie* theme of the tragic needs for pity and solidarity, became the centers of all the rest of Crane's great work. Except for a few poems, his future greatness was all to come in the short story. The one possible exception to that generalization would be *George's Mother*. In length it is a *nouvelle*, as Henry James called the form, at the most. But then, *The Red Badge* is hardly more; and one apologizes, if apology is ever needed, for the lack of complexity, of rich social involvement, which is the penalty *The Red Badge* pays for its superb compression, by noting that it too is perhaps a *nouvelle*. One does not expect of it what *Tom Jones* or *The Portrait of a Lady* offer.

With *George's Mother* Crane returns to the slums to tell the story of George's mother's losing fight to keep her boy uncorrupted in the Rum Alley neighborhood of *Maggie*. As she loses George to drink, delinquency, and a sure future as a Bowery bum, the mother loses her grip on life and slides away into death. The accent falls on George's confusion of values between home, mother, and church on one hand and street gang and saloon on the other. A more careful and mature study than *Maggie*, it lacks the dramatic intensity and compassion of Crane's first slum book. Brief, cold, and disillusioned, it focuses as much on George's cowardice as his bewilderment. It makes an interesting forerunner, Protestant and Old New York in viewpoint, of James T. Farrell's *Studs Lonigan*.

As this and all Crane's subsequent flights at the novel show, he did not live to grow into a mastery of manners which might have permitted the traditional novel, though he showed signs, especially in "The Monster," of growing that way. There is no surprise, given the circumstances of his last five years, in the fact that his three other efforts at the novel failed. The surprise lies in the greatness of the tales. It is, however, revealing to glance at these three attempts.

I

The Third Violet has by far the most charm. It came from a relatively happy and strong period of Crane's life, written in the midst of his perturbations over the success of *The Red Badge* and done because he wanted to do it—with some misgivings but *con amore*. It attempted to make use of Crane's experiences with painters and "Indians," and its hero, Hawker, was apparently more or less modeled on Linson. Crane had disclosed glimmers of capacity to dramatize manners in moments of *Maggie* and in incidental writings like "Mr. Binks' Day Off" and "An Experiment in Luxury." There is no doubt that maturity and adult experience would have ripened his powers to true mastery of the great tradition in the novel. But *The Third Violet* tends to show why novelists are seldom great before the age of forty. By contrast, it shows how youthful yet unique, how experimental yet inherently brilliant, Crane's best writing is.

The Third Violet, though exploiting autobiography, was a fascinating attempt to imitate W. D. Howells. The first part takes place in a resort like Hartwood, where Hawker has returned to his farm home to paint and where he sees and falls in love with Miss Fanhall at the summer hotel and courts her on the tennis court, on picnics, and on walks, with the help of his friend Hollanden, a cool Craneian writer. Howells, of course, had virtually invented the summer-vacation novel, had turned it into a *genre* convertible to all sorts of purposes, and had made its exploitation a steady part of his career. The other half of Crane's book was placed among the "Indians" of the Art Students' League Building. Howells, beginning with *A Hazard of New Fortunes*, was devoting much of his output in the 1890s to the problems of the artist in New York. *The World of Chance* had barely ceased publication in *Harper's Monthly* for November, 1892, when *The Coast of Bohemia* (which dealt in part with the students of the League before they moved out of their old Building) began to run in Bok's *Ladies' Home Journal* for December.

Crane of course knew and could do things Howells couldn't. Widely acquainted with painters, sculptors, architects of his own day, Howells knew Crane's generation best through his son, John Mead, and his daughter, Mildred. The impecunious "Comanches" of *The Third Violet*, fine portraits, and the model, Florinda "Splutter" O'Connor, a Maggie competent for survival, were as beyond Howells as the wonderful sketches of "Stanley"—a "large, orange and white setter." There are many fine touches in *The Third Violet* to prove that it was written by Stephen Crane: Hawker's perceptively studied farm folks; the Hartwood scenery; the Bohemians at home—"Wrinkle," "Great Grief" Warwickson, "Penny" Pennoyer, "Purple" Sanderson; and of course Splutter and Stanley. Those characters were all minor, however. It was in the perceptions of the real situations of the major characters and in the clarification of ideas to which those perceptions should have led that Crane fell down.

Probably it did not occur to Crane that Howells had spent thirty years learning how. Of course Howells, disillusioned of egalitarian myth, had discovered the broad drama involved in a situation like Crane's confrontation of poor, farmerish, gifted, artistic, personally superior Hawker with rich, urban, cultivated, sensitive but snobbish Miss Fanhall. It confronted two basic, fascinating American types, as Howells saw early: the "Social" and the common, the "conventional" and "unconventional," Society's lady and nature's gentleman. Over many years, with deepening perception and disillusion, Howells had studied the implications of all this until it had made an independent, semi-religious and democratic socialist of him. In *The Third Violet* Crane saw only personal injustice and amatory affront. Similarly, Crane wholly failed to dramatize the point Howells was making about the artist in a world of chance: that the combat conditions of a competitive, acquisitive society stifled art. Having the Bohemians just talk about it was not enough.

It was, however, only expressive immaturity, not seeing far enough, which held Crane back. Intrinsically, the situation he had imagined was far more immediate and dramatic in its potential, far more modern, than any comparable situation in Howells. After having Hawker woo Miss Fanhall in an inconclusive idyll, Crane transports him back to the city and a triangle. "Splutter" O'Connor, a "very honest" Irish girl with "a beautiful figure" frankly carries a torch for Hawker. Crane develops the setting, the *dramatis personae*, and the conflict in class, character, candor, and personal reality (much in "Splutter's" favor) between the two women—and then abruptly deserts it for a foggy final scene in which Miss Fanhall starts to brush Hawker off, as Hawker had done to "Splutter," and then incomprehensibly reverses herself and accepts him.

The failure to face and develop the conflicts of class and convention, of sex and of art against society, destroys the novel and strips its deficiencies of all concealment. Its fragmentary brevity, its lack of competence to carry off scenes requiring the full development of conversation, its confusion of ideas and missed opportunities of a dozen sorts, and its ultimate lack of achieved, over-all form protrude like the skeleton of a half-built house. And the key to all this failure may easily be seen on consideration to be Crane's entire inability to comprehend women, especially Miss Fanhall.

It was not necessary to her case that Crane should understand Maggie Johnson personally or even consider viewing her from within. Not explaining her either, he does a good introductory job of communicating the personality of "Splutter" O'Connor. But, as Carl Van Doren said of the women of *Active Service,* "with young girls [Crane] never outgrew the young man's sense that they are cryptic creatures, whose words never mean what they seem to say and whose silences are deeply mysterious." They are "incomprehensible."[1] That is everywhere true but triply so if they are ladies. Crane's ladies are just about what Lowell said of Fenimore Cooper's, "Sappy as maples and flat as his prairies."

That sappiness had some warrant in Howells, who had made a life-long study and some wonderful comedy of the vagaries of feminine logic, of the irresponsible emotionalities, and of the quixotisms of ladies full of a dangerous pride in the little knowledge they had gleaned from romances. Howells had not in several instances been above the trick, once his real story was told, of sugar-coating it for the hopeless magazine reader with a story-rounding "happy" ending based on such illogic—secure in the faith that perceptive readers would enjoy the joke and others would never feel the irony till they sneezed.

The real trouble with *The Third Violet* and *Active Service* is that, in dealing with women in fiction, Crane's irony deserted him. He did not have a clear single view of them, much less a double or triple vision. One of the difficulties, in fact, of accepting the recurrently popular notion that Crane's early "affairs" were more than the passion of the moth for the star, that he was a roistering whore-chaser, an experienced lover before Cora, a trapped exemplar of Freud's case of "A Special Type of Choice of Object Made by Men," is that none of this experience did anything for his imagination. If such experience existed, it was, among Crane's experiences, uniquely unavailable to his creative mind. The main exception, which is post-Cora, may appear in the troubled poem "Intrigue."

Except for the almost laughably romantic portrait of Nora Black, *femme fatale* and war correspondent like Cora, who was probably derived from Cora, Crane's women are imagined exactly as they might have been had he been quite innocent, quite normal. Perhaps he was. Marjory Wainwright of *Active Service* is portrayed no more sophisticatedly than Miss Fanhall. And Nora Black, as Carl Van Doren said, is handled "with a boy's ferocity. Snubs which would batter an ordinary woman into pulp only accelerate her pursuit of the cool hero. She is no less a myth than eager Venus on the trail of young Adonis."[2]

For the rest, it seems impossible to improve on Van Doren's criticism of *Active Service* as far as it goes. Beyond Van Doren, the significance of *Active Service* and Crane's part of *The O'Ruddy* lies in their revelation of the late, desperate, and pathetic struggle of Crane's integrity with bestsellerism. In the age of *Trilby*, *Graustark*, and *When Knighthood Was in Flower*, inferior literary talents coined money in such golden floods as had never before been won by authors. Cuban glory, an exasperated consciousness that his superior talent still earned far too little, haste, and that pressure of money for "Brede" which Ford and Liebling believed killed Crane, all tempted him to cash in on the fad. In pieces like "The Private's Story" and "The Clan of No-Name" he gave in occasionally to embarrassingly Kiplingesque ideas and mannerisms.

But his surrender was never for long. It seems that he wrote *Active Service* only because Harold Frederic insisted he must: it would be the salvation of his career. Frederic knew how to grind them out; Cora must hold Stephen to it. But if neoromanticism were to be his salvation, Crane was not to be saved. He could not resist the realist's game of inflating and then puncturing it. In *Active Service* he sends Coleman, the correspondent, to rescue Marjory Wainwright at the front. Coleman loves "reflecting upon the odd things which happen to chivalry in the modern age . . . he made no effort to conceal from himself that the whole thing was romantic" but took "a solemn and knightly joy in this adventure." As Crane builds it up, Coleman sees himself "dealing with a medieval situation with some show of proper form: that is to say, armed, a-horseback, and in danger, then he could feel that to the Gods of the game he was not laughable." He "took satisfaction in his sentimental journey. It was a shining affair. He was on active service, an active service of the heart . . . even as the olden heroes . . . he had never known that he could be so pleased with that kind of parallel."

Coleman prospers as Minniver Cheevy, however, no better than Henry Fleming had. At the first real danger he is lost: "He would not have denied that he was squirming on his belly like a worm through black mud," and yearning to get out. "If his juvenile and uplifting thoughts of other days had reproached him he would simply have repeated and repeated: 'Adventure be damned.' "

The same feelings motivated the design for, and the large fraction Crane lived to write of, *The O'Ruddy*. Crane's historical imagination was keen, but he never had confused things either by supposing that he could seriously re-enter the past or by lacking respect for the sense of the past because it was imaginary. Therefore to him the irresponsible historical romance was fair game. In *The O'Ruddy* he tried to write a sword-clashing, picaresque, true-love-laden, coincidence-packed romance *and* make fun of the silly, golden *genre* by burlesquing it with the best sustained humor he had yet achieved. All the life goes out of style and characterization when Robert Barr takes over. Barr's troubles were not, as he supposed, with plot so much as with focus of character, tone, atmosphere, and dialogue. If Crane had lived, *The O'Ruddy* might have been a brilliant *tour de force* on themes by the ghostly Stevenson.

II

After *The Red Badge*, then, Crane's aspiring novels are about what one would expect of a novelist his age: essentially autobiographical, occasionally intense, sporadically gifted, weak in characterization, fragmentary in form. A number of the short stories, on the other hand, are absolutely first-class; some of them are of definitive, classic stature. Bernard Berenson described them as "having almost Dante's or Tolstoi's gift of making one see the people and scenes he describes."[3] I suppose there is not much higher praise left to imagine. It is a measure of the greatness of the best that there can be space to discuss only those few and that the others, so very good, must be let go.

Widely anthologized as a standard representative of the short story and Crane's work, "The Open Boat" has too often been appreciated for biographical or tendentious reasons and too seldom for its authentic artistic power. The tale has repeatedly been called naturalistic, even the one pure American example of naturalism; or impressionistic; or the work of a symbolist, or even of an existentialist. And commentators have been peculiarly tempted to the exercise of the biographic fallacy—the identification of the author himself with the interior substance of the fiction—by the circumstances of the story's provenience. Crane *was* shipwrecked, spent long hours at sea in a dinghy, was swamped in the surf, and lost Billy Higgins coming ashore. He did write up all but the dinghy voyage for the *New York Press*, and wise anthologists have found it useful to print the account *seriatim* with the fiction. Crane (or Scribner's) did subtitle it: "A Tale Intended to be after the Fact. . . ."

"After the Fact" here may as well be in pursuit of the truth of experience as of the mere exact occurrence, however—and in Crane it is much more likely to be. Actually, "The Open Boat" seems one case in which a grasp of the methods of Crane the visionist, the perspectivist, reconciles difficulties. As most modern critics have seen, and as most undergraduates recognize on comparing the news report and the story, the latter is altogether a work of art. That being true, the biographical events were at best the occasions for the tale; it does not in the least matter that Crane may have made free imaginatively with the wind, weather, or anything else; and to identify Crane himself with "the correspondent" in the fiction is naïve.

The essence of Crane's art and achievement in "The Open Boat" is his control—subtle, complex, and intense—of its internal points of view. The famous opening line announces the centrality of point of view: "None of them knew the color of the sky." Why not? Their group point of view was concentrated on the never-ending athletic feat of surmounting each gray, snarling, "barbarously abrupt and tall" wave which tried to capsize their dinghy and drown them. That group viewpoint, uniting the men in a brotherhood of danger, is the first, least usual, and most important of three points of view in the story. The other two are that of the neutrally observing narrator, who reports dramatically on the scenes which occur among the men, and that of the intellectual in the boat, the correspondent. It matters immensely to an understanding of the story that one see through which point of view events are conveyed.

Crane's newspaper account has the fact-perspective of his journalism: strong in effects yet told in a flat, technically "objective," first-person narrator's voice. The significant thing about the fiction is that the major perspectives are those of the characters. They

know the human solidarity and the generosity (best shown by Billy
the oiler) of men whose eyes are cleared to see that they face death.
One of them has shifting fantasies, certainly psychological and
perhaps symbolic, as he rows through the darkness. At the end, with
Billy in his grave and themselves safely abed—"When it came
night, the white waves paced to and fro in the moonlight, and the
wind brought the sound of the great sea's voice to the men on the
shore, and they felt that they could then be interpreters."

It may be that the real implications of Cyrus Day's challenging
reconstruction of the nice day on which the *Commodore* sank, and
of the ethical problems of Captain Murphy, are that "the facts," the
actualities of his open-boat experience were so ambiguously
bathetic that Crane made no attempt to transcribe them. He set to
work to imagine it as a trope of man's condition face to face with
nature, fate, and death. At any rate, the story certainly is such a
trope. This being true, the polarity of points of view in the story is
all important. If Stephen Crane can ever be unmistakably shown to
be a symbolic naturalist, it is in "The Open Boat." But to prove him
so is to exercise the biographic fallacy and identify him with the correspondent and his thoughts with the correspondent's thoughts. For
it is in the correspondent's mind and point of view that the key symbolic perceptions occur in the story. But does the story believe in his
symbols?

Rowing all alone in the darkness with the others plunged in exhausted sleep, the correspondent begins to think in Section VI of
the story: "If I am going to be drowned . . . why . . . was I allowed to come thus far and contemplate sand and trees?" The voice
which succeeds is that of the summarizing neutral narrator. But
what he summarizes is so placed in the framework of the correspondent's reveries that it is unmistakably the substance of the
correspondent's thought. He thinks that to drown him would be
"an abominable injustice" and a "crime most unnatural" to a man
"who had worked so hard, so hard." And then it occurs to him that
"other people had drowned at sea since galleys swarmed with
painted sails," and he is led to reflect despairingly on the quality of
what is natural and where man stands:

When it occurs to a man that nature does not regard him as important,
and that she feels she would not maim the universe by disposing of him, he
at first wishes to throw bricks at the temple, and he hates deeply the fact

that there are no bricks and no temples. Any visible expression of nature would surely be pelleted with his jeers.

Then, if there be no tangible thing to hoot, he feels, perhaps, the desire to confront a personification and indulge in pleas, bowed to one knee, and with hands supplicant, saying, "Yes, but I love myself."

A high cold star on a winter's night is the word he feels that she says to him. Thereafter he knows the pathos of his situation.

This reflection is, of course, not unrelated to the collective point of view of the men in the boat. They had earlier, upon not quite daring to try the surf on the beach, rejected the idea that the "old ninny-woman, Fate," might dare to drown them. And the narrator comments that this present content of the correspondent's thought, while discussed by nobody, had no doubt been reflected upon by each man "in silence and according to his mind." It is nowhere suggested, however, that the correspondent's conclusions are those of the group. On the contrary, when in the morning they head for the beach again and see the white windmill, Crane explicitly gives it to the correspondent to see it symbolically. "It represented in a degree, to the correspondent, the serenity of nature amid the struggles of the individual—nature in the wind, and nature in the vision of men. She did not seem cruel to him then, nor beneficent, nor treacherous, nor wise. But she was indifferent, flatly indifferent."

"The Open Boat" gains its greatest force, then, from a metaphysical tension between two opposing possibilities of the meaning of the death of Billy the oiler, as these possibilities are registered in the two kinds of character perspective. In the correspondent's point of view naturalism is almost classically presented. Nature is flatly indifferent, man will lose his struggle to survive; nature is therefore implicitly contemptuous and hostile; and man is absurd and the proper object of self- (since none else can feel it) pity. This gives rise to the naturalistic tragedy of pathos and bathos.

The opposing possibility, implicit in the heroism, the generosity, and the death in victory of Billy, implies of course a wholly opposite set of conclusions. The most admirable man in the boat, whose life is laid down for his friends, Billy is certainly no less a Christ-figure than Melville's Billy Budd. His function in the story seems much more obviously Christ-like than Jim Conklin's in *The Red Badge*. He plays the greatest part in creating the human solidarity, the brotherhood, the capacity for real pity, the disinterested "love of Being in general" which makes man in the story anything but absurd. Billy dies, but he gets his comrades safe to shore. The implication is that man by courage and complicity can rise superior to the pathos of his situation; he can understand it and answer it with the magnificence of his defiance, his acceptance, and perhaps even his use of it to achieve a classically tragic elevation.

The tension between these two polar possibilities is left unresolved in "The Open Boat." For readers, certainly the complexities raised by that tension make for experience of a far higher order than the merely naturalistic, as may be seen by comparing its effects with those of the ending of Hemingway's A *Farewell to Arms*. That remains true even if one ends by declaring for the naturalistic interpretation. I think, however, that Crane in this one of the greatest of his short stories meant the same sort of ambiguity to stand as that which we find in the greatest of Hawthorne's short stories. Tension stands, and courage and negative capability are essential until one finds, as Crane never did, a way to resolve it.

III

The second of Crane's unmistakably great short stories, "The Blue Hotel," has also stirred a vortex of warring criticism much of which no longer matters. Though some of the symbol-hunting has ranged past the point of the ludicrous, that criticism has not left much of the story unexplored. The comments of Joseph Satterwhite and Stanley B. Greenfield are particularly helpful.[4] In much of the criticism the most striking feature is the resolute explaining away of portions of the text in order to make the story conform with the critics' predetermination that it shall be a work of naturalism. Actually, however, "The Blue Hotel" is no more purely naturalistic than any of Crane's other major work.

It tells the story of the irruption upon the sleepy little town of Fort Romper, Nebraska, of a hysterical foreigner, a Swede, who turns up at Scully's Palace Hotel in the midst of such a raging blizzard as Crane had seen scourging the farmers on his Western tour. Moody and jittery, announcing that he knows he will be killed, the Swede challenges the hospitable instincts of the hotelkeeper. Scully bucks him up with liquor and good fellowship, whereupon his guest turns insufferably arrogant. There is an uneasy card game which leads to a fist-fight between the Swede and Scully's son. Victorious and more arrogant than ever, the Swede checks out of the hotel, swaggers down the street to a saloon, tries to force the local gambler to drink with him, makes the mistake of manhandling the gambler, and is stabbed to death. In a final scene two of the other erstwhile guests of the blue hotel, the cowboy and the Easterner, talk the tragedy over.

There is no evidence in the story that it is nature or any other deterministic force which kills the Swede. No "force" compelled him to come to Fort Romper, and certainly none compelled him to mistake it for the Wild West. The cowboy's exasperated objections to the delusive quality of the Swede's perceptions are well taken. But it is apparently Crane's *donnée* that a lifetime of dime-novel romanticism about the West shall be a condition of the Swede's neurosis. Crane neither asserts nor denies that such romanticism may in itself have unhinged the Swede. He merely gives us an unhinged foreigner mad with the conviction of his impending death, his compulsion to find it, and a fixation upon violence which is properly only fictional. As we should now say, the Swede is a perfect example of the self-fulfilling prophecy.

One of the most intriguing factors in the story is the blueness, the shrieking, outrageous saturation of the color of Scully's Palace Hotel. What does that represent? A really satisfactory answer might provide one a key to all Crane's famous use of color and color words. But one of the most interesting things about all the criticism is that nobody appears to have found the key either to the general question or to the specific case. This suggests that perhaps there is no key. Perhaps Crane found color significance where he found it, pluralistically, on an *ad hoc* basis, without a generalizable or theoretical ground for what he did.

Most obviously, the hotel's business is commercial. Nobody passes the town on the train or enters the town from the train without seeing, remembering, and perhaps entering the blue hotel. Beyond that, one can read all sorts of significances into the defiance of that color. It may be man's "coxcombry" against the blizzard of the universe, that conceit which is "the very engine of life." It may be for old Scully, the one quite human being in the story, the assertion of his humanness. On the other hand, it may be the Swede's rejection of humanity for that frantic, romantic dream which brings him the "purchase" of his death, or it may be the failure of the other men to join Scully's effort to treat the Swede as a man and brother which makes them complicitly guilty of his death.

For some readers, the story has seemed properly to end at the
conclusion of Section VIII, where, "The corpse of the Swede, alone
in the saloon, had its eyes fixed upon a dreadful legend that dwelt
atop of the cash-machine: 'This registers the amount of your
purchase.' " The final section, IX, has been a scandal and a stum-
bling block to no few commentators partly because it challenges a
simply naturalistic reading of the story, partly because it explicitly
introduces a moral idea and militates against the notion that Crane
is always a nonideological symbolist in his art. Actually, what the
addition of that final page and a half does to the story is greatly to
enrich it by deliberately reversing its moral perspectives and restor-
ing them to the same challenging ambiguity between naturalistic
and at least humanistic perspectives of "The Open Boat."
When the silent little Easterner suddenly breaks silence to explain the situation to the cowboy, naturalistic symbols, at-
mospheres, and ironies are totally missing. The language, the irony,
and the symbolic drama are now moralistic; the sanctions behind
them are humanistic if not religious. As a matter of fact, the
perspective of the Easterner is that of Christianity as interpreted by
Tolstoi and no doubt mediated to Crane through Howells. This is
the language, just as it is the strategy of presentation, of that doctrine of complicity which Howells had been developing in book
after book during the ten years before Crane left New York for
Cuba. "We are all in it!" says the Easterner, ". . . every sin is the
result of a collaboration. We, five of us, have collaborated in the
murder of this Swede. Usually there are from a dozen to forty
women really involved in every murder, but in this case it seems to
be only five men—you, I, Johnnie, old Scully; and that fool of an
unfortunate gambler came merely as a culmination, the apex of a
human movement, and gets all the punishment." And the cowboy,
to point up the irony, is given the line behind which every one
would like to hide from the searching finger of his complicit guilt in
the world: "Well, I didn't do anythin', did I?"
If one reflects back—as Crane clearly intended one should—from
this point across the whole of the preceding story, he sees that this is
not an appendage upon the tale: it provides another point of view.
Though it has not been popular to do so, one might have read the
story of the Swede as one does the stories of so many of the
characters of Stephen Crane's great contemporary, Edwin Arlington
Robinson. Perhaps the Swede was a kind of combination of Minniver Cheevy and Richard Cory. Or, of course, as it has been most

popular to show, the Swede's story might be one of symbolic naturalism. The final section of "The Blue Hotel" provides a third perspective, one without which the story is far less significant than the great work Crane gave us. It seems hardly necessary to detail all the implications of that multiplicity. No criticism of the story, however, can finally be taken seriously which confines itself to less than the full complexity of its perspectives.

IV

"The Open Boat" and "The Blue Hotel" are the sort of intense stories of masculine adventure, action, tragedy, and irony which it is generally agreed that Stephen Crane did supremely well. There has been too little tendency to grant him also the power to deal with the homely, domestic, and commonplace tragedies of society and the ironic examination of manners which have characterized American realism at its most typical and best. It was toward this which he must have grown had he matured into an achieved mastery of the novel in its traditional forms and concerns. It was this toward which he must have matured if he were to have matched Robinson or Joyce in his own way. But there has been too easy an assumption that, because the financially desperate and physically dying Crane of his last eighteen months obviously declined in creative power, his genius had actually preceded his body in death, his talent been burned out.

In the premises, of course, no such assumption is necessary. And actually Crane showed in some of the later writings great promise of proceeding toward the perceptions and problems necessary to his maturing. Such development may be seen in "The Monster," in "The Bride Comes to Yellow Sky," and in the best of the *Whilom-ville Stories*. In these for the first time in Crane one is moving toward a dense, adult, demonstratedly complicit society. The great vein of the major novelists, the novel of manners, is beginning to open. Crane's is a world not only of young men and children but of grown men and grown, non-chivalric, and comprehensible women. It is not surprising that Crane turned to the exploitation of the *genre* of the boy book which had been developed by the American realists. But it was less to be expected that he should now take up the theme which Twain and Howells had prepared for Crane's generation—especially Cather, Anderson, and Masters—the theme best labeled by Sinclair Lewis's original title for *Main Street*, "The

Village Virus." In Whilomville and in Yellow Sky the terror and the beauty of the American small town's security and boredom and vulnerability are as beautifully portrayed as they would be by any of the specialists to come.

If he did not temperamentally suspect it before he went, Stephen Crane spotted the secret of the romantic West the moment he got there. And he told it delightfully in "The Bride Comes to Yellow Sky." The secret which Roosevelt, Wister, and Remington would not let themselves believe was not only that the Wild West of romance did not exist but it never had. Natty Bumppo and all his descendants had been *beaux idéals*, privileges of the romancer. Romance was always somewhere, sometime else. "This ain't Wyoming, ner none of them places," says a "deeply scandalized" cowboy in "The Blue Hotel," "This is Nebrasker." The best the frontier could offer were the raw, hoodlum tests of courage of "A Man and Some Others" or "Horses—One Dash." Courage was always splendid—but what tested it might be evil, stupid, or merely absurd. The reality of the West, of the frontier, is the exorcism of chimeras like Scratchy Wilson by the mere advance of social realities like the marriage of the marshal to a commonplace little waitress from San Anton'. The proper mode of dealing with the theme was comic, that of social comedy, and Crane hit it perfectly in his story.

The same sense of social reality dominates the non-mythic stories of initiation which Crane told of the boys in Whilomville. The best of these—"The Stove," "The Knife," or "His New Mittens"—throw a good deal of light on "The Monster," the major work Crane imagined from the same setting. Here Crane begins with what at first looks like a fairly ordinary Stephen Crane concern for the nature, conditions, quality, and fate of heroism. But he proceeds within a uniquely dense web of multiple characters and social reference. The compact descriptions of the substance and quality of the life of the village in its many social levels are brilliantly effective. The accuracy of Crane's sense of all sorts and conditions of men, women, and children is unexpected in the author of the almost abstracted characters of *Maggie* and *The Red Badge*. Crane never lets go of this exploration in a new, social context of his themes of courage and heroism; but, by the time one is half way through the story, he has become aware that the title is as essential and as pregnant as that of a poem by George Herbert.

Briefly, the story is that of Dr. Trescott, whose Negro stableman is horribly burned, mutilated, and reduced to idiocy in rescuing

Trescott's son from a fire. Whilomville's first reaction to this, when it thinks Henry Johnson is going to die, is a sensational, romantic exaltation of his heroism. Trescott labors, with his own heroic devotion, to save Henry's life. But he cannot save his mind or his face. Gradually the sentiment of the town swings to revulsion against the poor derelict. Trescott, however, will neither forget nor cancel his debt of admiration and gratitude. Hysteria mounts. By the end of the tale, Trescott is suffering professional boycott and social ostracism for sheltering a monster.

The question becomes, Who is the Monster? And by the time one is done pondering the elements and implications of scene and action, he comes to a chilling conclusion. Everybody is. This is true in some sense for every individual character, at every social level, in the village. And it is true for the village as a whole. In fact, by the end the village itself, especially in its most respectable and dominant society, is most particularly the monster. Crane has never had to editorialize, but the indictment is colder, more furiously returned than in any comparable work. "The Monster" cries out for a more adequate criticism than it has received. But Berenson thought "The Monster" was "finer even than Ibsen's *Enemy of the People*, because here the people do their best to ruin a man who, out of loyalty and humanity, refuses to discard a person whom they cannot abide in their midst—well written as well as thought out."⁵

V

Like pluralistic views of Crane's approaches to life and literature, appreciation of this latter development of his imagination spoils the harmony of a simple, unitary view of what he was and could do. It also challenges the notion of a burned out Crane whose death was no real loss to American letters. On the contrary, one remains convinced that the loss of Stephen Crane was a real tragedy to the development of our literature, our culture. A. J. Liebling put it well: "I think, myself, that Crane might have written long novels of an originality as hard to imagine, in retrospect, as *Maggie* and *The Red Badge* would have been to anticipate."⁶ Among the men, Crane's death and then that of Frank Norris left his generation of novelists reduced essentially to Theodore Dreiser. Whatever one thinks of Dreiser's genius, it is clear that it could have profited immensely from the context of real contemporaries as gifted as Norris and Crane. And I, for one, think that Crane's gifts ranged widely beyond and above those of Dreiser. The tragedy of Crane's early silencing, quite apart from any element in it personal to Crane, is that of the death of any gifted young person. It is the tragedy of the unperformed, the unrealized, the never to be known.

In the end the real power of Stephen Crane is in awareness, the power to register and to make the reader see what he saw. Regardless of qualifiers, of what the vision saw, he is supremely a visionist. The one greatest unfairness dealt him has been the repeated implication that it was romantically himself he was trying to make the reader see. On the contrary, the essence of his art was to give, in his characters, persons with eyes and to set them in turn within perspectives which would let readers see both very sharply and complexly around them and so to feel life as Crane felt it. That is true of every great artist. It is equallly true of them all that, having felt their power, one must decide for himself how far to accept it. Crane's vision was preternaturally "modern" in its progression to irony. Accept it or not, no honestly hospitable reader can deny either the power of its artistic transmission or, therefore, the youthful yet permanent greatness of Stephen Crane.

Notes and References

Because of their frequent occurrence, several standard works are identified by brief citations as noted below:

Work *The Work of Stephen Crane.* Ed. Wilson Follett. Twelve vols. New York: Alfred A. Knopf, Inc. 1925 - 1926. In the light of the extensive Crane editing of the past half-century and more, perhaps the most significant parts of this first collected edition are the introductions by authors, some of whom knew Crane personally, especially Joseph Hergesheimer, I; Robert H. Davis, II; Carl Van Doren, IV; Amy Lowell, VI; Willa Cather, IX; Charles Michelson, XII.

Virginia Edition *The University of Virginia Edition of the Works of Stephen Crane.* Ed. Fredson Bowers. Ten vols. Charlottesville: The University Press of Virginia. 1969 - 1975. With due allowance for controversy, supersedes all previous editions. Where in the notes below reference is made to Crane writings in obscure newspapers, I think in all cases the texts may readily be located in *Tales, Sketches and Reports,* VIII. But, for the reader who wishes only to see where and when, I have preserved reference to the original publication, which in many cases I found in the large, bibliographically pioneering collection of photostats gathered by the late Lester G. Wells.

Letters *Stephen Crane: Letters.* Ed. R. W. Stallman and Lillian Gilkes. New York: New York University Press, 1960.

Linson Corwin K. Linson, *My Stephen Crane.* Ed. E. H. Cady, Syracuse: Syracuse University Press, 1958.

Crouse *Stephen Crane's Love-Letters to Nellie Crouse.* Ed. E. H. Cady and Lester G. Wells. Syracuse: Syracuse University Press, 1954.

Gilkes Lillian Gilkes, *Cora Crane: A Biography of Mrs. Stephen Crane.* Bloomington: Indiana University Press, 1960.

Beer   Thomas Beer, *Stephen Crane.* New York: Alfred A
Knopf, Inc. 1923.

Chapter One

1. Crane to Ripley Hitchcock (1896?), *Letters,* p. 119.
2. Linson, p. xiii.
3. For specific reference to the Crane scholars cited here, see
"Selected Bibliography," pp. 171 - 73.

Chapter Two

1. One of Crane's conscious professional masks was that of "the
youthful stranger with the blonde and innocent hair". As often happens
with regard to artistic *personae,* however, one runs quickly up against
the question of how much that same "New York Kid" was a mask and in
what degree he was at least an aspect of the real person.
2. Joseph Conrad, "Introduction," to Beer, pp. 6 - 10.
3. Though especially as "popular culture" the ideal of the
American gentleman needs a thorough study which would produce a
significant book, we have made a start in Edwin H. Cady, *The
Gentleman in America* (Syracuse, 1948), and Stow Persons, *The
Decline of American Gentility* (New York, 1973).
4. *Letters,* p. 119.
5. "Stevie," *New York Evening Literary Review,* July 12, 1924.
6. *Crouse,* p. 11.
7. "The Merry Throng at Hot Springs,"*Philadelphia Press,* March 3,
1895.
8. L. U. Pratt, "The Formal Education of Stephen Crane,"
American Literature X (January 1939): 461.
9. *Crouse,* pp. 2 - 4.
10. "The Merry Throng at Hot Springs."
11. Charles Michelson, *Work,* XII, pp. xii - xiii, xvii - xix.
12. *Letters,* p. 319.
13. John D. Barry, editor of *Forum,* thought so; and Barry was
apparently more actively impressed by Crane's "lines" than anyone
else at the moment.
14. The terribly difficult business of dating both this and *The Red
Badge* has been clarified by Donald Pizer, "The Garland-Crane
Relationship," *Library Quarterly* XXIV (November 1960): 75 - 82.
15. For variations on this text as taken from different newspaper
subscribers to the Bacheller Syndicate, see *Virginia Edition,* VIII, pp.
418, 884 - 86, 1013.

16. Linson, p. 86; *Letters,* pp. 56, 58.
17. See especially T. F. O'Donnell, "Notes on the Reception of Crane's *The Black Riders,*" *American Literature* XXIV (May 1952): 233 - 34.
18. *Letters,* p. 73.
19. *Crouse,* p. 29.

Chapter Three

1. *Crouse,* p. 42.
2. *Letters,* p. 106.
3. Ibid., p. 107.
4. Cf. Floyd Dell, "Stephen Crane and the Genius Myth," *Nation* CXIX (December 10, 1924): 637 - 38.
5. See Crane to Wm. Crane, Nov. 29, 1896, Barrett Collection. Cf. *New York Journal, World, Times,* September 17, 1896; *Press,* Jan. 5, 1897; and scraps of another Crane account of the affair, Clifton Waller Barrett Collection, University of Virginia.
6. See Stephen Crane Scrapbook, Barrett Collection.
7. Gilkes, p. 26.
8. Ibid.
9. *Letters,* p. 138.
10. Cf. Cyrus Day, "Stephen Crane and the Ten-foot Dinghy," *Boston University Studies in English* III (1957): 193 - 213.
11. Cf. E. R. Hagemann, " 'Correspondents Three' in the Greco-Turkish War . . ." *American Literature* XXX (November 1958): 339.
12. "Stephen Crane at Velestino," *New York Journal,* May 11, 1897.
13. "That Was the Romance, The Red Badge of Courage—a Story. This Is the Reality, A Battle Today in Greece—A Fact," *New York Journal,* undated clipping, Syracuse University Library, Stephen Crane Collection.
14. Cf. *Virginia Edition,* V, 125, 139.
15. John Bass, "How Novelist Crane Acts on the Battlefield," *New York Journal,* May 23, 1897.
16. Quoted in Linson, p. 103.
17. See Thomas F. O'Donnell and Hoyt C. Franchere, *Harold Frederic* (New York, 1961), pp. 65 - 68.
18. Gilkes, pp. 109 - 10.
19. Beer, pp. 160 - 61.
20. This guess rests on the letter of E. L. Trudeau to Cora Crane, *Letters,* p. 184.
21. *Work,* Vol. XII, p. xiii.
22. "Sayings of the Turret Jacks . . ." *World,* May 15, 1898.

23. "The Red Badge of Courage Was His Wig-Wag Flag," *World,*
July 1, 1898.
24. *Notes of a War Correspondent,* 1911, p. 125.

Chapter Four

1. *Bookman* I (May 1895): 229.
2. Harvey Wickham, "Stephen Crane at College," *American
Mercury* VII (March 1926): 293 - 94.
3. Stephen Crane pocket notebook, Barrett Collection.
4. *Letters,* p. 110. Cf. n. 31, p. 109, for provenience.
5. In general, see Cady, *The Gentleman in America,* on the history
of this phenomenon.
6. See *Crouse,* pp. 30 - 52.
7. See esp. Russel Roth, "A Tree in Winter: The Short Fiction of
Stephen Crane," *New Mexico Quarterly* XXIII (Summer 1953):
188 - 96; and Max Westbrook, "Stephen Crane: The Pattern of
Affirmation," *Nineteenth Century Fiction* XIV (December 1959):
219 - 29.
8. Beer, p. 140.
9. *Crouse,* p. 63.
10. *Scenes and Portraits: Memories of Childhood and Youth* (1954),
pp. 124 - 25.
11. Cf. Helen R. Crane, "My Uncle, Stephen Crane," *American
Mercury* XXXI (January 1934): 26; and Robert H. Davis in *Work,* Vol.
II, p. xvii - xix.
12. *Virginia Edition,* V, 50.
13. *Virginia Edition,* VIII, 746.
14. "Signalling Under Fire," cf. *Virginia Edition,* VI, 195 - 96, 198,
199 - 200.
15. Letter in the Howells Papers, Houghton Library, Harvard.
Published by permission of the Trustees, Remington Art Memorial,
Ogdensburg, New York, and of The Houghton Library, Harvard
University.
16. Cf. *Letters,* pp. 31, 62, 93, 127.
17. Cf. Remington's enthusiasm for "a romantic literature in America
and an art . . . the most romantic of all," in *Letters of Francis Parkman,*
ed. by Wibur R. Jacobs, 1960, II, 225.
18. "With Greek and Turk: I. An Impression of the 'Concert,' "
Westminster Gazette, June [9?], 1897.
19. "My Interview With Soldiers Six," *New York Journal,* June 20,
1897.
20. "The Blue Badge of Cowardice," *New York Journal,* May 12,
1897.

21. "Stephen Crane and Julian Ralph Tell of War's Horrors . . . ," *New York Journal*, May 23, 1897.

22. "How They Leave Cuba: Stephen Crane Describes a Sad Sight," *New York Journal*, October 6, 1898.

23. By T. A. Gullason, "New Light on the Crane-Howells Relationship," *New England Quarterly* XXX (1957): 389 - 92.

24. "Stephen Crane Says: Edwin Markham Is His First Choice for the American Academy," *New York Journal*, March 31, 1900.

25. Beer, p. 205.

26. "Hunger Has Made Cubans Fatalists," *New York World*, July 12, 1898.

27. *New York Sun*, May 17, 1896.

28. Beer, p. 140.

29. "With Greek and Turk: VII, The Man in the White Hat," *Westminster Gazette*, June 16, 1897.

30. "Stephen Crane Fears No Blanco," *New York Journal*, August 31, 1898; "Stephen Crane in Havana: He Sees the Comic Side of Things," *New York Journal*, October 9, 1898.

31. "Stephen Crane Says: Watson's Criticisms of England's War Are Not Unpatriotic," *New York Journal*, January 25, 1900.

32. "Regulars Get No Glory," *New York World*, July 20, 1898.

33. "Coney Island's Failing Days," *New York Press*, October 14, 1894.

34. "How They Court in Cuba," *New York Journal*, October 25, 1898.

35. *Crouse*, pp. 30 - 32.

36. Linson, p. 37.

37. "Mr. Binks' Day Off: A Study of a Clerk's Holiday," *New York Press*, July 8, 1894.

38. *War Is Kind*, No. XXV.

39. "Ancient Capital of Montezuma," *Philadelphia Press*, July 21, 1895.

40. *Work*, II, 205 - 6. Cf. *Virginia Edition*, VI, 205 - 206.

41. *Crouse*, p. 33.

42. Beer, p. 140.

43. *New York Press*, April 29, 1894.

44. "Coney Island's Failing Days."

Chapter Five

1. In Melvin Schoberlin, ed., *The Sullivan County Sketches of Stephen Crane* (Syracuse, N.Y., 1949), p. 19. See also James B. Colvert, "The Origins of Stephen Crane's Literary Creed," *University of Texas Studies in English* XXXIV (1955): 179 - 88. The ten "Sullivan County

Sketches" published by Schoberlin are, following finds by Prof. Thomas A. Gullason and by Prof. Stallman, expanded in number to nineteen in the *Virginia Edition*. See Vol. VIII, pp. xxi - xxxii, 847 - 61.

2. Cf. Cady, *The Big Game*, passim.

3. Beer, p. 140.

4. See Donald Pizer, "Crane Reports Garland on Howells," *Modern Language Notes* LXX (January 1955): 37 - 39.

5. Cf. E. H. Cady, *The Realist At War: The Mature Years, 1885 - 1920, Of William Dean Howells* (Syracuse, N.Y., 1958), pp. 212 - 18.

6. "Realists Must Wait," *New York Times*, October 28, 1894.

7. Robert Stallman, ed., *Stephen Crane, an Omnibus* (New York, 1952), p. 14.

8. Gathered from the *San Francisco Wave*, July 4, 1896, in Maurice Bassan, ed., *Stephen Crane's Maggie: Text and Context* (Belmont, Calif., 1960), p. 114.

9. *Maggie: A Girl of the Streets. A Story of New York*, ed. Joseph Katz (Gainesville, Fla., 1966). In critical discussion I have quoted the text of this facsimile.

10. "New York Low Life in Fiction," 1896; "Dialect in Literature," 1895, are both collected in Cady, ed., *Howells As Critic* (London, 1973). The quotations come, successively, on pp. 258, 236, 259.

11. In "Stephen Crane: *Maggie, A Girl of The Streets,* " in Hennig Cohen, ed., *Landmarks of American Writing*, Voice of America Forum Lectures, 1970, pp. 193 - 202.

12. *One Year's Reading For Fun* (New York, 1961), p. 15.

13. "Stephen Crane Scholarship Today and Tomorrow," *American Literary Realism* VII (Spring 1974): 127, 129 - 31.

14. *Letters*, p. 40.

15. James M. Cox, *"The Pilgrim's Progress* as a Source for Stephen Crane's *The Black Riders,"* *American Literature* XXVIII (January 1957): 478 - 87.

Chapter Six

1. *Last Essays* (1926), p. 122. Cf. J. B. Colvert, *"The Red Badge of Courage* and a Review of Zola's *La Débâcle,"* *Modern Language Notes* LXXI (February 1956): 98 - 100.

2. See H. T. Webster, "Wilbur F. Hinman's *Corporal Si Klegg* and . . . *The Red Badge of Courage,"* *American Literature* XI (November 1939): 285 - 93; E. Solomon, "Another Analogue for *The Red Badge of Courage,"* *Nineteenth Century Fiction* XIII (June 1958): 63 - 66; M. Klotz, "Crane's *The Red Badge of Courage,"* *Notes & Queries* VI (February 1959): 68 - 69. Cf. E. Stone, "Crane's 'Soldier of the

Legion,'" *American Literature* XXX (May 1958): 242 - 44.

3. See A. Feldman, "Crane's Title from Shakespeare," *American Notes & Queries* VIII (March 1950): 185 - 86; C. D. Eby, Jr., "The Source of Crane's Metaphor, 'Red Badge of Courage,'" *American Literature* XXXII (May 1960).

4. Wickham, 295.

5. *Work*, X, 200. Cf. Katz, *Maggie*, 126.

6. Wickham, 293.

7. See esp. T. F. O'Donnell, "De Forest, Van Petten, and Stephen Crane," *American Literature* XXVII (January 1956): 578 - 80; and "John B. Van Petten: Stephen Crane's History Teacher," *American Literature* XXVII (May 1955): 196 - 202.

8. *Work*, I, pp. xi - xii.

9. See *New York Tribune*, January 20, 1897, and *Rochester Post Express*, February 22, 1897 (Stephen Crane Scrapbook, Barrett Collection) commenting on H. D. Traill, "The New Realism," *Fortnightly Review*, January 1, 1897.

10. "Editor's Easy Chair," *Harper's Monthly* CVII (June 1903): 146 - 50.

11. "Life and Letters," *Harper's Weekly* XXXIX (October 26, 1895): 1013.

12. Bass, op. cit.; "With Greek and Turk, III," *Westminster Review*.

13. See Arthur Golden, ed. *Walt Whitman's Blue Book*, Vol. I. *Facsimile*. New York, 1968.

14. Barrett Ms, p. 65. Cf. Stallman, *Omnibus*, p. 276.

15. Barrett Ms, "SV" p. 75 on verso of "LV" p. 118; "SV" p. 76 on verso of "LV" p. 97; "LV" p. 85. (Cf. Stallman, *Omnibus*, pp. 291 - 92).

16. Barrett Ms, "SV" p. 84 on verso of "LV" p. 113; p. 85 on p. 108; p. 86 on p. 112. (Cf. Stallman, *Omnibus*, pp. 298 - 300).

17. Barrett Ms, p. 125. (Cf. Stallman, *Omnibus*, p. 317).

18. Winifred Lynskey, "Crane's *The Red Badge of Courage*," *Explicator* VIII (December 1949): 18.

19. See James Nagel, "Stephen Crane and the Narrative Methods of Impressionism," *Studies in the Novel* X (Spring 1978): 76 - 85. The essay may be supposed to adumbrate his forthcoming book on Crane and impressionism.

20. *Willa Cather on Writing* (1949), pp. 35 - 43.

21. "War Memories," [December 1899] *Work*, IX, 245 - 46.

22. Joseph J. Kwiat, "Stephen Crane and Painting," *American Quarterly* IV (Winter 1952): 331 - 38.

23. Linson, pp. 46 - 47.

24. *Work*, IX, 201. *Virginia Edition*, VI, 222.

25. *Stephen Crane: Selected Prose and Poetry*, 1950; rev. ed., *Stephen Crane: "The Red Badge of Courage" and Selected Prose and*

Poetry (New York, 1956; third edition, 1968), p. v.

26. Charles Feidelson, *Symbolism and American Literature* (1953), esp. pp. 44 - 76.

27. *Work*, Vol. I, p. x.

28. *Modern Language Notes* LXXV (February 1960): 111 - 13.

Chapter Seven

1. *Work*, IV, p. xii.

2. *Work*, IV, p. xi.

3. Berenson, p. 23.

4. Stanley B. Greenfield, "The Unmistakable Stephen Crane," *PMLA* LXXIII (December 1958): 562 - 72, and Joseph Satterwhite, "Stephen Crane's 'The Blue Hotel': The Failure of Understanding," *Modern Fiction Studies* II (Winter 1956 - 1957): 238 - 41.

5. Berenson, p. 19.

6. A. J. Liebling, "The Dollars Damned Him," *New Yorker*, August 5, 1961, pp. 48 - 72.

Selected Bibliography

THE BRIEF ESSAY UPDATED

The first edition of this book so nearly antedated the rise of the Crane field that it could discuss "six basic books indispensable to the study of Stephen Crane" and presume to annotate a list of some 65 other really prime sources. The essay on basic books even launched judgments and predictions which the years have somewhat vindicated. Since 1960, however, Crane bibliography in most of its phases has taken quantum leaps forward. To treat of the field adequately would monopolize more than the space available in the volume. Still worse, to replicate the method of the past would, on the whole, simply reduplicate work done amply and well by others. It is obviously much more sensible to list the best of the helps to Crane study.

We still need a definitive volume devoted to the primary bibliography of Crane manuscripts, printing and publication histories and descriptions, memorabilia and ana. Nevertheless, the brief Crane section in the second volume (pp. 329-38) of Jacob Blanck's great *Bibliography of American Literature*, 1957, is helpful; and there is a world of information scattered through the ten volumes of Fredson Bowers, ed., *The University of Virginia Edition of the Works of Stephen Crane*.

Aids to secondary bibliography are now incomparably ampler than in 1960. Since the first in 1963, *American Literary Scholarship, An Annual*, edited in variant patterns of alternation by James Woodress and J. Albert Robbins, has provided selections and annotations done by teams of selected scholars. Experience with all such helps, however, suggests that the student ought never to think that he can substitute a commentator's remarks for his own reading of an article. Nobody ever pretended that such reliance could be made sure. Beyond *ALS*, look to the annotated *Hawthorne, Melville, Stephen Crane: A Critical Bibliography* (N.Y., 1971), the Crane section done by

169

Stanley Wertheim. Not only maturer but informed by deeper knowledge are the two best bibliographical essays in the field: "Stephen Crane," by Donald Pizer in Robert A. Rees and Earl N. Harbert, eds., *Fifteen American Authors Before 1900: Bibliographical Essays on Research and Criticism* (Madison, Wis., 1971); and Joseph Katz, "Afterword: Resources for the Study of Stephen Crane," in Joseph Katz, ed., *Stephen Crane in Transition: Centenary Essays* (Dekalb, Ill., 1972). Both are indispensable, and the new student should pay attention to what they agree in saying about R. W. Stallman, *Stephen Crane: A Biography* (New York, 1968).

Of the volumes gathering commentary on Crane, the most useful seem to be *Stephen Crane's Career: Perspectives and Evaluations* (New York, 1972), edited by Thomas A. Gullason; and then Richard M. Weatherford, ed., *Stephen Crane, The Critical Heritage* (London, 1973), which limits itself to commentary made during Crane's lifetime or just afterward.

The latest major contributions to the field appear in Hershel Parker, ed., "Special Number on Stephen Crane," *Studies In the Novel* X (Spring 1978): 182 pp. It publishes Henry Binder's defense of his theory of *The Red Badge of Courage* text and a discussion of the textual illogicalities of the *Virginia Edition's Maggie* by Hershel Parker and Brian Higgins. Still more important are David J. Nordloh's general estimate: "On Crane Now Edited: The University of Virginia Edition of *The Works of Stephen Crane*"; then Donald Pizer's magisterial bringing up to 1978 the essay he did for Rees and Harbert, this new one called, "Stephen Crane: A Review of Scholarship and Criticism since 1969." Students will also find a harvest of Pizer's long, gifted consideration in the readings attached to his Norton Critical Edition of *The Red Badge of Courage*, 1976.

What has otherwise occurred most strikingly during the past two decades has been the emergence of deeper, more illuminating studies of the age, the foregrounds and backdrops to Crane's thought, life, art—the milieu, as Hippolyte Taine called it. Among major books are Warner Berthoff, *The Ferment of Realism: American Literature, 1884 - 1919*, 1965; Larzer Ziff, *The American 1890's: Life and Times of a Lost Generation*, 1966; Jay Martin, *Harvests of Change: American Literature, 1865 - 1914*, 1967; Ellen Moers, *Two Dreisers*, 1969; Howard

Mumford Jones, *The Age of Energy,* 1971; Edwin H. Cady, *The Light of Common Day,* 1971; Donald Pizer, ed., *American Thought and Writing, The 1890's,* 1972; Daniel Aaron, *The Unwritten War,* 1973; Edwin H. Cady, *The Big Game: College Sports and American Life,* 1978.

For the immediate future in Crane studies we urgently need the definitive primary bibliography, the sufficient biography, and a textually noncontroversial edition of the work; but most of all we need readings of Crane for the new age which is upon us— a fresh, mature, and applicable body of criticism.

Index

Adams, Henry, 77, 78, 79, 96, 124
Adams, Samuel Hopkins, 22–23
Åhnebrink, Lars, 75–76
Alden, Henry Mills, 45, 88
Aldrich, Thomas Bailey, 28, 111–12
Anderson, Sherwood, 125, 157

Bacheller, Irving, 46–48, 49, 50, 58, 60, 61, 127
Barr, Robert, 150
Barrett, Clifton Waller (and Barrett Collection, University of Virginia), 16, 22, 25, 118, 127
Barrie, J. M., 62
Barry, John D., 45
Bass, John, 125
Bassan, M., 106
Battles and Leaders of the Civil War 20, 43–44, 118, 119
Becker, C., 22, 56, 72
Beer, Thomas, 17, 25, 31, 33, 55, 56, 68, 75
Bellamy, Edward, 91
Berenson, Bernard, 110, 150, 159
Berlin, Sir Isaiah, 26
Berryman, John, 17, 25, 55, 58, 68
Bible, The, 38, 96–97, 102–103, 115–16
Binder, H., 25
Bowers, Fredson, 16, 23–24, 109
Brooks, Van Wyck, 84
Bruccoli, Matthew, 16
Bunyan, John, 114
Bushnell, Horace, 27
Button, Lucius, 21
Byron, Lord, 56

Cahan, Abraham, 107
Cartwright, Peter, 27
Cather, Willa, 48, 133, 136, 157
Charvat, W., 24

Christian Gentleman, The, 30–32, 81–82, 99
Christianity, 77, 79, 80, 84, 99, 108–109, 113–16, 137–38, 153–54, 156
Clark, Dora, 56–58
Claverack, 34–37, 119
Colvert, James B., 16
Commodore, The, 52, 60–61, 103, 152
Conrad, Joseph, 31–32, 66, 71, 73, 82, 118, 133, 134
Cooper, Fenimore, 35, 47, 82, 84, 123, 148, 158
Crane, Agnes, 29, 30
Crane, Cora, 22, 56, 58–60, 61–62, 63, 65, 65–67, 70–71, 72–74, 148–49
Crane, Edmund, 39, 41, 50, 73
Crane, Jonathan Townley, 27, 28–29, 30, 33, 34, 38, 80, 81
Crane, Mary Helen Peck, 27, 29, 32–34, 35
Crane, Stephen

LIFE (for summary see "Chronology")

WORKS
"Ancient Capital of Montezuma," 49
Active Service, 36–37, 58, 63
"An Experiment in Luxury," 97, 146
"An Experiment in Misery," 97
Black Riders, The, 42, 46–47, 49–50, 53–54, 54, 55, 80, 113–16
Blood of the Martyr, The, 93
"Blue Hotel, The," 98, 104, 154–57, 158
"Bride Comes to Yellow Sky, The," 66, 103–104, 157, 158

172